Correction of the Ego/Spirit Mind (Learning That All Roads Lead to Rome)

May this book be a guiding inspiration to you on your journey here on earth as a Spiritual being experiencing a human journey, while you are seeking True Spiritual potential and advancement.

Rev. Mercedes Pepe, O.M.C.

Correction of the Ego/Spirit Mind

ISBN 978-0-578-06166-5

Printed in the United States of America

Correction of the Ego/Spirit Mind (Learning That All Roads Lead to Rome)

Rev. Mercedes Pepe, O.M.C.

Power Technology Publishing Co.
www.powertechnology.org

Dedication

To my Pop, Angelo Quiles; I only wish it would not have taken so many years to share our knowledge of Universal Oneness. I would have never guessed through the years of trials and tribulations as a child and teenager that we were spiritually on the same page. I'm grateful that at the end of your life here on earth we could experience and share forgiveness, knowledge and love, laying down illusions of what we made up about each other and recognizing each other as Spiritual Oneness.

<u>Acknowledgement</u>

Thank you to my loving husband, Clement Pepe who supported and championed me to write this book; who also spent many hours assisting me in putting this book together. I also would like to thank my loving daughters, Danielle and Natalie for believing that Mama could do anything she sets her mind to, and for embracing the work that I do.

Also, to my beloved dog Angel who passed during the completion of this book. My faithful loving companion, I miss you but I know we will meet again.

Contents

Correction of the Ego/Spirit Mind

Introduction

This book has been given to me from Spirit through automatic hand writing. I never had to think it out, I just took pen and paper and the writing began. Prior to the writing I had a dream in which I would write a book called "Correction of the Ego/Spirit Mind." As a Spiritual Teacher I feel this is a gift from God, to be received through me to you. It is based on reaching higher consciousness for our self and humanity. It not only gives explanation of the *split mind* known as ego thought versus Spirit thought system, but it also provides how to take action on the correction of the illusionary *split mind* for higher levels of consciousness. It is based on different modalities of Spiritual wisdom I have read, studied, taught and lived over the past two decades of my life. I only wish I grew up knowing all of this sooner, but I now realize that it was and is part of the classroom journey we Spiritual beings encounter through our thoughts, and that life is the condition of our thoughts in which we create an illusionary unconscious walking dream we perceive from day to day.

I have put together a way to help rid the mind of negative ego thoughts and redirect them toward the Spiritual mind, which exists within all of us. Our mind is not created as a dual mind; it is our thoughts of duality that creates it to appear separated from Oneness. In future chapters I will discuss this more. For now, let's concentrate on healing our mistaken ideas of what we perceive to be real as our painful identity, instead of the Creative Power Source of our True Identity and Universal Oneness with God, the same God that is within

Correction of the Ego/Spirit Mind

us waiting to express the full super conscious mind through humanities growth and consciousness.

Let us seek to change and heal the condition of our thoughts through Spirit mind thinking, allowing ego thoughts to fall away. How will this happen? By the way we feel. If you feel bad you have chosen the ego, if you feel good you have chosen Spirit to guide you. It's a simple concept but a little complex when living in a world of collective consciousness of illusion. I have answers on how to assist you toward living these concepts, now that you are ready and open to the great possibilities of self realization as your Spiritual center, as Rome was once the center for all roads.

With practice and work you will exercise your daily Spirit thoughts until they become automatic to you, like when you go to a familiar destination and can't remember how you got there but there you are. We can do this with our everyday thinking, if we learn and practice the same familiarity it took us to learn any other auto pilot thoughts we have.

Remember, knowing the ego mind thinking and the Spirit mind thinking is always gauged by how you feel about perceived circumstances. If you're feeling angry, sad, fearful, upset (ego mind). If you're feeling joyful, peaceful, loving, forgiving (Spirit mind). Choose to manage your *split mind* away from ego mind to Spirit mind, and it will change the way you feel about yourself and others and lead to a higher consciousness.

Thank you for receiving the Workbook: Correction of the Ego/Spirit Mind. I am now going to explain how to best use the workbook and how you can receive the benefits it has to offer, in retraining the mind to an advanced place of peace and happiness. It really works but you need to work it by actually doing the processes provided in the workbook. Each time you complete a process you move up the ladder to a higher consciousness of your True Spiritual Self. By the end of Chapter 16 you can have a major shift in your life take place. Do not judge your progress, everyone advances at different stages. *Judgment in any form causes discomfort and pain as do opinions. If we rely on everyone else's opinions we would not have any of our own.* So take the journey at your own pace and receive what's possible for your Spiritual growth and understanding.

Blessings,
Rev. Mercedes Pepe, O.M.C.

Correction of the Ego/Spirit Mind

These are key words used in this workbook. You may want to familiarize yourself with them for better clarity and understanding of how I apply them throughout the workbook.

Ego: Distinguishing itself from others. A part of the thought system.
Spirit: Holy Trinity. Inherited good qualities of the thought system.
Split Mind: Separated into two parts of the one mind.
Illusionary: Imaginary; the appearance of something made real.
Universal: Space present everywhere.
Oneness: Identity and unity.
Wholeness: A complete system.
Conscious: Intentional awareness.
Subconscious: Buried deep within the mind, and not aware of.
Super-conscious: Thinking above the conscious, to higher levels of the
        mind.
Dualism: Two parts of one.
Singular: As being one part.
Wholeness: A complete system not divided.
Collective: Singular, but being one part of a group.
Archetypes: A primordial collective unconsciousness within the
        psyche, acquired by the human race through time.
Divine: Supremely God.
Truth: Accurate, not being of a false nature.
Journey: Travel from one place to another.
Creator: To make and bring about.
Trans-state: Not fully aware, deep in thought.
Energy: Power source.
Power: Authority, strength.
Eternal: Forever being.
Human Being: A Spiritual being inside a dense body as a vehicle in
        which to be seen.
Spiritual Being: Spirit self; a moving soul's identity.
Observation: To watch over and take notice.
Perception: Presides thought; also known as a belief.
Realization: A condition of being aware.

Correction of the Ego/Spirit Mind

Chapter 1

Correction of the Ego Mind

Have you ever wondered who you are? Where did you really come from? Where are you going? What is your Universal Purpose? Well I have, and in many years of searching and studying Eastern Religions, Western Religions, Science of Mind, Course in Miracles, Kabbalah etc., I believe it all comes down to the Universal Truth of One Mind, One God that we are all a part of, and that we have simply forgotten our Truth. All the great books have been handed down to us for better understanding, but what sometimes happens is we misunderstand according to our own misconceptions and believing knowledge as being outside of us, in an exterior World, rather than inside the interior of who we really are.

How do we achieve this? We can pray, meditate, read and understand Scripture, process, mind train, Spiritually awaken hypnosis etc. All of which we will cover in this book. We just need to implement them long enough to stop the ego mind chatter and listen to our Spiritual inner voice.

There is a super powerful consciousness within all of us that leads us to the same inner peace of being at one with God. It's as if we are little outlets that plug into an Almighty Energy. How many of us use our outlets wisely? We plug in nightlights, TVs, computer games, etc., but there is something else very important that needs to be plugged in daily. That's our analytical decision making mind, that has been given free choice between Spirit and ego thought system.

How does one know when they have chosen the ego thought system? Easy, it simply does not feel good. That's your first clue. However, Spirit thought system is going to feel good. You will have a sense of freedom and empowerment, simply because you chose wisely. If we could look past our short circuit programs based on past

Correction of the Ego/Spirit Mind

recordings in our mind and realize that each day, hour, minute and moment is a chance to make a new choice, by first going to our Spirit decision making mind instead of automatic reactions based on fears.

Well that sounds great, but how does one do that. That's why we're going to take an overview of Spiritual teachings and practices, in order to come back full circle to the truth of who you really are. We are of One mind but because of past conditioning we have created dual personalities; right mind thinking and wrong mind thinking, Spirit versus ego, angel on one shoulder, and devil on the other shoulder. Where does this all come from? How did this get created? Let's start with the human mind, also known as the computer, the camera, the recorder of the body; where all the knee jerk reactions come from, starting from the moment of birth and perhaps before.

I believe it was Freud who said, "From the moment we are born we begin to die." One of the reasons he may have said that is because we come into life in such a dramatic way. We are experiencing pushing and pulling, cries of labor pains from mother as we are leaving the womb. We may have heard sounds that we hadn't yet understood but later would hurt our subconscious mind. If all goes well during delivery we're fully alive and innocent. What we know about our recent experience in the womb and perhaps before, we can not communicate in speech at the time of our birth. If we could communicate at that time we might be able to tell all the secrets that we spent lifetimes to learn. On some level we have chosen the parents, siblings and experiences this body will have in this lifetime. We chose this at the time of complete wholeness and in pure Spirit. We believed we could take on these challenges and were even excited about it.

Once born into the world, amnesia sets in and we soon forget why we came here. It then takes us a lifetime of learning to remember what is our contribution to Humanity and the reason why we are here. Eastern philosophy and some metaphysical philosophies believe many lifetimes will occur until we get it right, and at that time we decide to stay in Spirit form remaining closer to the Oneness of God.

Whatever our beliefs are there is the Soul's energy within us that is longing for love, that we can only truly give ourselves first from the God that lives within us; whose likeness we are created in.

What is this amnesia? Why do we forget our purpose once born into this world? The reason is because once we enter the human body and into the world an inherited dualistic mind takes over. We learn how to manipulate the world around us. At first our little mind tells us we are hungry, wet, thirsty, need to be held. As our caretakers care for our needs we see that a cry of demand gets us what we want; fed, changed, held. It takes very little time to get this down, if I want I get, it's a perfect system. Until one day the little mind gets split into a dual way of thinking, which is: "I'm not hungry, thirsty or wet, but I want to be held, if I cry loud and hard enough my caretaker will have to hold me. I'm happy when I'm held, then I'm more happy when I'm held and song to, then I'm more happy when I'm held, song to, and being tickled and rocked," etc. We learn quickly in our mind to want more, which is inherited from the moment we arrive here on Earth. Our caretakers quickly tire of our demands. We hear and feel resentment from others, as it comes to us as perceived negative subconscious thoughts. The unloving look on our caretakers face, the words of frustration they may speak. What happens here is our act is no longer cute. The caretakers have their own perceptions of how the caretaking will take place.

So, the two individuals that once worked together as one begin to split into two separate thought systems, which are: "I'm right you're wrong, I lose you win, visa versus." Why does this happen? Because we have what's called, ego mind thinking; that must always try to make itself right about a situation. It so wants to be right that it looks for evidence wherever it can find it. Within the mind is the one side of the illusionary split mind called the ego, which will go to any length for survival. It records negative perceptions to defend itself and give itself purpose for survival. It then collects and records a store house of thoughts, feelings and memories in which to call on for defensiveness, grievances and justifications of negative perceptions. This starts with the people we come in contact with, which are usually our caretakers. As we begin to develop we live into our basic instincts of survival. Some call this time the terrible twos. At this time we are working the system even more to see what we can and can not get away with. Now, with growing up come the permanent imprints in the Mind. As we grow up the reason we get nervous, upset, and angry generally comes from an earlier similar experience. It is hardly ever just the present moment. It's a push button that goes into our pre-recorded ego mind of survival. From there the ego mind goes into automatic suggestion of thought: "I am being attacked, survive survive," cries the ego mind, and up comes the files of evidence from earlier similar times of upsets. Frequently this goes on through childhood, adolescence and adulthood, sometimes costing us education, health, jobs and meaningful relationships, etc.

Correction of the Ego/Spirit Mind

Most important of these are the meaningful relationships; when we once again become related to a person much the way we were related to our caretakers. These meaningful relationships are the closest we will be to a Spiritual human being; this is not only the place where our buttons from the past are easily pushed but also where our most amount of healing will take place. For each person brings not only their wounds but also their need for healing these wounds. Through open communication and attentive listening we can learn about each other's early perception of life and help one another out of the past and into the present moment. This is called, "knowing one's pain condition." We all have them; no one leaves childhood without them.

When we share responsibly what happened, not our perceived story about what happened through possible misperceptions and opinions of what we experienced happening, we set ourselves free from the past. The difference is most stories are based on lots of our opinions and assumptions that the subconscious ego system uses to remain a victim. To remain a victim is fear of not surviving and to not allow Spirit and forgiveness to take the lead to empowerment and a new creative thought system which is always there for us to tap into.

Not that I'm dismissing some very traumatic and painful experiences any of us have encountered, but using Spirit thought system to perceive and learn can take our journey from victim to hero. Ego thought system will always choose victim in order to keep its identity, for without it we would come to know ourselves as God created us, pure Spirit. Anything else is a perception of the world we see in which we think is outside ourselves.

True salvation lies within our mind, the one mind that thinks as God created us to think in oneness and not in duality. The thought that we live in a dualistic world is in our own perception of separation from the Oneness of God. What it really comes down to is that the world is based on the meanings we put to each situation that occurs. Our meanings are chosen from either the ego mind system or the Spirit mind system.

Process

Underlying Ego thought and Belief Handling

1. What ego thoughts do you have about yourself?

2. Where did you develop these thoughts?

3. Who or what contributed to these thoughts?

4. What feelings are generated through these thoughts?

Correction of the Ego/Spirit Mind

Now take the questions to the Spirit Mind and ask:

1. What Spirit thoughts do you have about yourself?

2. Where did you develop these thoughts?

3. Who or what contributed to these thoughts?

4. What feelings are generated through these thoughts?

Split Mind

Let's now explore split mind and how it came into existence. For that we will go to the Biblical version of mankind's creation to circa 2100 BC. In the beginning there was God, God spoke the Word that created the heavens and the earth. God took the formless empty darkness and said: "Let there be light," and there was light. God separated light from darkness. Light and darkness have always been represented as a dualistic idea to us, not only from day to night but also with our thoughts. Although it may seem to be separated, day and night come from the Oneness of God, who we may think coexists with the universe but is in Oneness with the universe, for He is the Alpha and the Omega, the Beginning and the End. The belief is that the cycle of life is a continual process of teaching and learning the Oneness that we are. In some cosmic way we are all connected, always working to remember and restore humanity to it's consciousness of Oneness.

There was a time when we made up our own small individual ego mind with a need to survive in a dream world that was made up from a split mind that forgot its oneness. Was it a fact that we were told to leave the Garden of Eden after partaking of the fruit of knowledge, or was it a misperception or an opinion that God separated from us because of the guilt and shame we felt? How can God separate from Universal Wholeness, that would be duality and duality is not what God is. God is Oneness! It could only be in our own split mind which may have taken place at the moment of a wrong decision to want more of what we already had and all that we needed. Free choice has always been given to us but it has always been our responsibility to be the cause rather than the effect. All that may have been needed in the garden was a correction to thinking back to the Oneness, but by giving it power, guilt and shame we made the separating real to the illusionary ego mind and from there it continued to collect evidence of our sinful and guilty nature. We separated from our True Source, God. <u>God would never separate from us.</u>

Process

1. In what areas of your life do you feel separation?

2. What areas of your life do you feel a sense of Unity?

Dualism

We later have the account of Cain and Abel, the dualistic idea of good and evil. Abel offers up to God the best of his flock, as he is a herdsman. Animal sacrifices were common place at that time. Today we have what's called tithing, 10% of our earnings, towards where we experience the Spirit of God at work. What exactly Cain's offerings were I'm not sure for he worked the soil and brought forth fruit to God that may not have been the best of the bunch, for he felt God was displeased with him. Cain became angry and down cast so much that he later said to his brother Abel: "Let's go out to the field." There in the field Cain attacks and kills his brother Abel. How is this possible to take place in a Universe of Oneness? Well, perhaps that Oneness is a Universal agreement between Cain and Abel to play two sides of the same coin. A metaphor about how the split mind works when wrong mind thinking is chosen. Before that God said to Cain: "If you do not do what is right, sin will be at your door, for it desires to have you, but you must master it."

What we have is One Master Mind with the false belief of a separated mind. If God is Good, Faith, Spirit and Oneness how could he know about sin and separation? Therefore, it is in the mind of what we think within our own individual small selves, separated from God, instead of one with God and the Universe. Our real salvation lies in attuning ourselves to the True Intelligence that created us in It's Own image. The question to ask now is: Do we address God as Male or Female? This brings us back to the Oneness we all are, God's Energy, which has no duality. This Energy is both Male and Female, as we are also. We just have chosen a physical form of female or male for our life lessons here on Earth. Our Spiritual teachings have always contained male and female; Adam and Eve, Isis and Osiris, Mother Mary and the Son Jesus.

As it has been said; So man will take a wife and both shall become one. The number one signifies new beginnings, oneness with God, a Unity of Life. Oneness and wholeness is our hearts true desire, we have a natural instinct to couple our energy with someone, even though we contain this energy within ourselves. When two create a covenant it builds two pillars between an alter. Not that anyone who finds themselves single is anything less, for in such cases one uses their own reserve of male female energy, and still makes their contribution to Humanity. Contribution meaning, we are not meant to

9

live and die in vain, we are here to be a living demonstration of God's Oneness with Our Universal Connection.

Process

1. How do you show your demonstration of God's Universal Oneness?

2. How would you like to show your demonstration of God's Universal Oneness?

Chapter 2

All Roads Lead to Rome

As we study, learn and teach the Universal Knowledge that is our inherited Gift, we come upon different paths leading to the same destination. Remember, we are working with Universal Oneness. Because we are at different stages at different perceived times in our lives, our existence of study and learning comes at what seems like different intervals. One person may be studying Kabbalah, traditionally known by some as the world's most esoteric source of Spiritual knowledge, with fascinating teachings about our relationship to God, in that everything is in divine order and that there are no coincidences. Everything happens for a reason toward our guidance to learn; our part we will play in this script called life here on Earth, and how letting go of our ego thought system will bring us closer to the Universal Oneness of God, which is that Great Almighty Energy Source that we plug into. The Kabbalah belief is that there are thirty two celestial paths of wisdom from which the world was created with number, speech and story. In the Bible we have stories which are the Word (speech). The number of days God took to create and rest (number), Adam and Eve (story).

Once again I approach the word story, a tale of something through the perceiver's thoughts. Traditional story telling was oral and handed down generation after generation until the written stories came to be. My belief is once stories are told from one person to the next, a perceived translation takes place when that story is written and rewritten then translated into different languages such as: From Hebrew/Aramaic/Greek/Old Latin, etc; different slants and interpretations along with one's perceived ideas may take place. Even a scribe could have his own perception, even though they were well trained to translate written words as written.

The word Kabbalah literally means: "To that which is received." It can be received through a theoretical thought system, meditation, or reaching a higher consciousness through the practice of Yoga. We can see how important it is to channel energy into our minds as well as our physical body. Our hands are used in prayer, blessings, receiving and giving. They correspond with the number ten. Five fingers on one hand, five fingers on the other hand. This is called the "sefirot," which is both masculine and feminine. On the left we use the feminine, starting with the thumb which is called Binah, then to Gevurah, Hod, Yesod, ending with the baby finger Malkhut.

Binah: Understanding the Oneness of God's Almighty Energy.

Gevurah: Courage to have the strength in your own knowing.

Hod: Glory to God's Oneness.

Yesod: Foundation of our own beingness.

Malkhut: Kingdom over all of nature's domain.

On the right side is the Masculine, starting with the thumb Keter, Chakhmah, Chesed, Tiferet, ending with the baby finger Netzach.

Keter: Crown of our communication with God's Oneness.

Chakhmah: Divine wisdom.

Chesed: Mercy for all that is divine in oneness.

Tiferet: Beauty that comes with Spiritual knowledge.

Netzach: Victory, being victorious in our Spiritual well being.

Put these ten fingers together uniting your palms, brought to your lips where you give speech, you create a covenant for your tongue to speak from the one self you really are, God's Wholeness. Biblically this was how blessings were given and received, and is still a ritual that is practiced today. Next time there is a telecast of the Pope watch his hands carefully as he appears before the people, or when you're in church, temple, or a monastery, watch the Spiritual leaders bring in the God Energy.

We perceive our individual identity to be so different but they all come from the same Source. It is written biblically in Revelations: "I

Correction of the Ego/Spirit Mind

Am the Alpha and The Omega, the Beginning and the End," says the Lord God, Who Is, and Who Was and Who is to Come, The Almighty."

I believe that the Almighty Spirit is in all of us. Our delusional mind perceives that there are many different roads but there is really one true road, and that direction is within us. If we quiet the mind chatter, take the time to pray/meditate and come from a place of possibility of faith, not from agreeing or disagreeing but from what's possible. Then, try that road, if it doesn't feel right then go on to the next road, it's still going to get you to that Spiritual place, as long as you follow the Universal Law of Oneness and release yourself from egotistical dualism of I'm right and you're wrong. Consciousness of our true self united as one Universal Energy Source will be our true salvation for happiness and fulfillment. That same happiness and fulfillment that our earthly mind thinks we have lost but haven't.

There is still much to explore with the Kabbalah and if it's something that has sparked your interest you will find many books written for more study on the subject. So for now, I'll stay with a simplistic overview. We can look at the Kabbalah as a mathematical Spiritual Thought System determining the numerical value of words and names.

There are twenty two Hebrew alphabets and ten sefirot. The ten sefirot can also be counted on the feet with ten toes, add the tongue and sexual organ, along with the ten fingers, discussed earlier, makes up twenty two elements of a God created body, who received the breath of God through the nostrils. So we are pure Spiritual beings on a human journey learning and earning our way back to the Spiritual realm in which we have forgotten is our true essence. The Scriptures are filled with symbolic words, names and numbers. In Genesis, Jacob wrestles with God and is told at daybreak that his name will no longer be Jacob, but Israel, because: "you have struggled with God and with man and have overcome." Israel stands for the name of an entire nation. We all have our inner demons to wrestle with. This again, is in our illusionary mind. Spirit mind is calling us to answer only to the One Mind of the Universal God.

Process

1. List your illusionary inner demons you wrestle with.

2. Flip your illusionary inner demon thoughts to Spiritual thoughts. Write down what comes to you.

Our Calling

I believe when we receive our calling there are times it becomes a great struggle to have faith and belief that the calling is a Universal energy working through humanity for a higher consciousness that is needed. Throughout the Bible we find people's names being given or names being specifically changed to another name, such as Abram to Abraham.

There were calculated measurements for Noah's ark, number of days the ark was to be on water, number of years the Israelites were in the desert. Two tablets containing the Ten Commandments called in Deuteronomy the Tablets of the Covenant. Why not one tablet? Because Moses was old and it would have been too heavy for him to carry? No, I don't think so. When two become one it becomes a unifying covenant appearing in a dualistic form but actually being singular in Spirit, much the way Spiritual Beings on this human journey appear to one another.

Until we seek to own and master our Spiritual Covenant with our Universal Oneness we will not hear the calling or know that it is Spirit speaking to us. This also is how our mind works, and what appears as dualistic ideas regarding split beliefs. Two thoughts can not occupy the same space at the same time. One will cancel out the other. For example: If your conscious mind wants to encompass all Spiritual beliefs to a singular idea that all roads do lead to Rome, Rome being the Universal Truth of Oneness, but your subconscious mind calls in all your feelings, such as: "Hell and damnation, it sounds like a lot of dogma I had to sit in church or temple to listen to when I was growing up, etc." What happens is our individual ego conflict on Spiritual belief systems takes place.

In essence a *split mind* comes into play in which nothing is understood from a higher conscious point of view, because our conscious mind thinks, and our subconscious mind feels. So, if they are simultaneously in opposition, one will cancel out the other and we will remain in a Spiritual quandary, in which no decisions are made and no Spiritual advancement takes place. Or, the subconscious ego thought system may go to: kill or be killed, I'm right and you are wrong, thinking it to be right while indulging in dualistic specialness of righteousness. This kind of thinking is what creates wars, both in the world and in our mind. The idea of oneness would have us look at what's possible in this systematic concept God has for us.

16

Process

1. List any and all quandaries (2 opposing thoughts on the same subject) in your life.

2. List the action steps it will take to remove you from the quandary and move you to your desired results.

3. Take the action steps and record your results.

Story

I love the story of two students who are in a theological disagreement and ask for the Rabbi to settle it. He listens to one student and declares you are right. Then listens to the other student's point of view and declares you are right. A third student listening in says, but Rabbi they both can't be right, and the Rabbi answers, you're right. The phrase, can we agree to disagree means it's all made up and we put the meaning into everything with our perception of thoughts, and this is what our Biblical stories repeat to us over and over again.

Let's look at the story of Moses in Exodus 3:13-15. God said to Moses: "I Am Who I Am, this is what you are to say to the Israelites: I Am has sent me to you." God is speaking of Universal Oneness, but once again Mankind is misperceiving through the Great Illusionary dream of separation. Egyptians Hebrews, are we not part of the Great I AM?

Perhaps we can see again the two sides of the same coin playing out a message, an enactment of right mind thinking and wrong mind thinking. Moses is the Leadership for God's chosen people, right mind thinking, and Pharaoh is the leadership for the Egyptians, wrong mind thinking, since his thoughts lie in separation that Egyptians should rule and Hebrews be slaves, along with his fear of them becoming too numerous to keep them oppressed.

Moses thoughts are on freeing his people, taking them to the land of milk and honey. Now, remember that God the I Am is orchestrating this, for He has chosen Moses. Moses declares to God, I am slow of speech and tongue. God then empowers Moses with a Staff (The Hand of God), which is always within us, and also granted Moses a spokesperson, his brother Aaron. Whenever two or more are gathered in the Oneness of God, miracles occur. Moses is reluctant to take on this mission because of his insecurities of speech and tongue. How many of us have harbored insecurity about ourselves in one way or another that has kept us imprisoned or enslaved from something greater within ourselves and for Humanity?

Pharaoh's part in all of this demonstrates the struggle we have with God (Right Mindness). How our hearts harden and our eyes see only material manifestations of life. We can read the Biblical Scriptures from a literal perception which makes it very harsh and ugly, or from a metaphoric perception in which we connect the dots with that One Wholeness in Mind, coming full circle to the truth of who we really are, and what our Spiritual purpose for humanity is.

Process

1. List your insecurities.

2. List your Spiritual securities.

3. What actions can you now take through your thoughts of Spiritual security?

More on Kabbalah

Kabbalah is said to contain the secret keys to higher understanding of the Spiritual Laws of the Universe, and the effect it has on the physical world to received fulfillment. A traditional belief of Kabbalah is that Moses understood these Spiritual Laws handed down through Noah, Abraham, Jacob and Isaac. Each time God moves toward the correction of humanity, Spiritual Laws are implemented, and each time something looks like opposition it is really one in the same. (One coin, two sides)

Among more modern people who studied these Spiritual Laws of cause and effect were Albert Einstein and Sir Isaac Newton. There is also the sacred text called the Zohar who some say is the backbone of Kabbalah, and the ancient mysterious Sefer Yetzirah, said to be a meditation text which contains magical overtones. It has also been written that the Sefirot is frequently referred to as the tree of life, the center line from Keter and Malkhut found on the human body in a Spiritual form.

Correction of the Ego/Spirit Mind

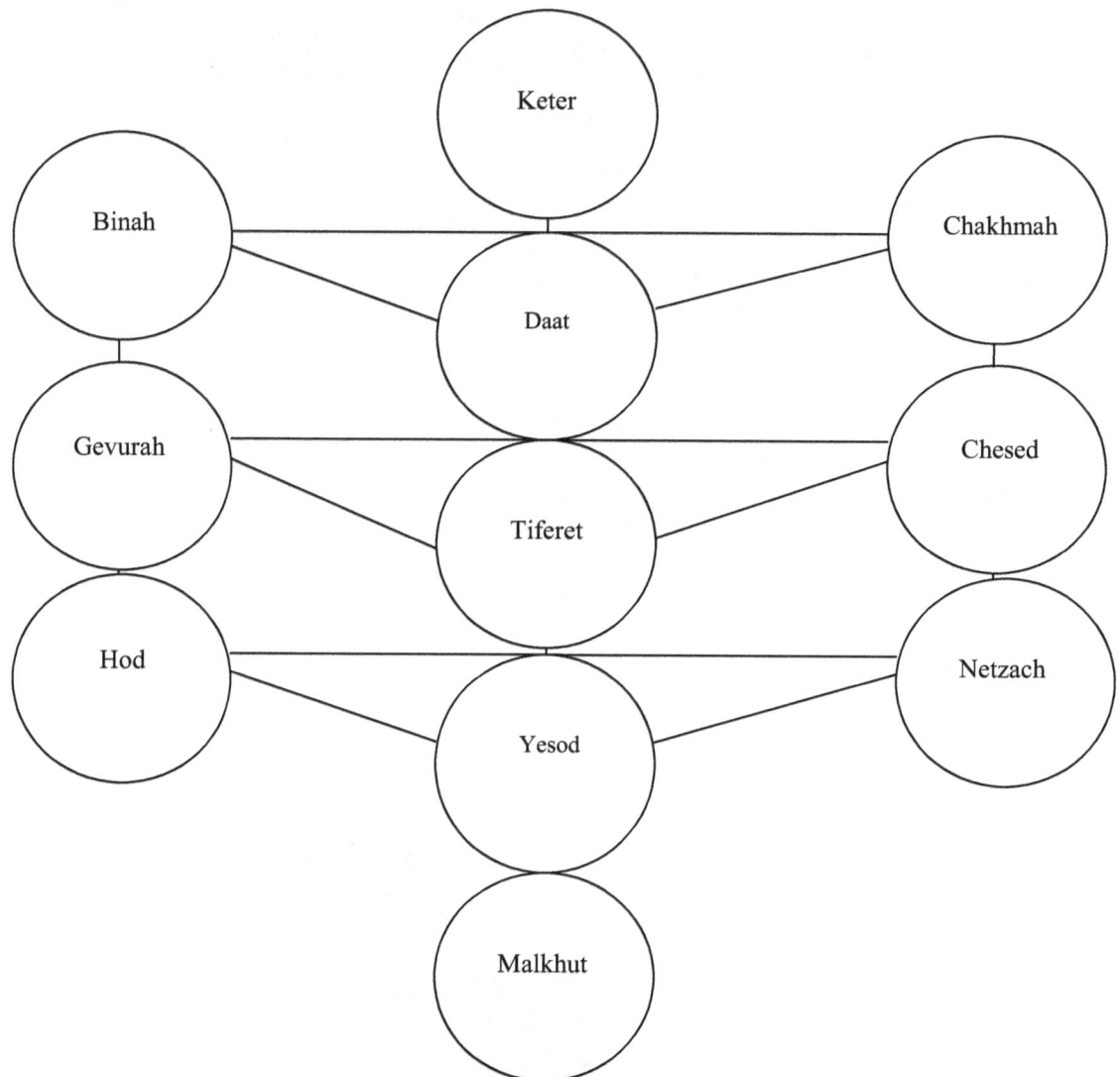

Keter

Binah

Chakhmah

Daat

Gevurah

Chesed

Tiferet

Hod

Netzach

Yesod

Malkhut

The Tree of Life

The diagram of the Tree of Life is a representation. Keter is of higher energy, Malkhut of lower energy. Later Kabbalistic beliefs place both energies in the Daat, the center also known to us as the third eye, the eye that sees beyond the form. That which is above is below, once again one mindedness.

The Tree of Life is climbing the Tree of Knowledge with the ten Sefirot, eleven if one were to count the Daat. The Tree of Life was our first initiation to split mindedness. In Genesis God did say, "You must not eat fruit from the tree that is in the middle of the garden and you

22

must not touch it, or you will die." How can we die if we are as God, eternal? We can't, only in our mind have we come to believe this illusion.

I believe what God was saying was you are of the highest consciousness of all creation because you are made in My Image and any level of lower consciousness will split your mind into the illusion of separation and death. In that split moment in time we went into a continual cause and effect of dualism. Paradise lost within the mind, who thinks it is a separate entity from God.

Process

1. List the ways you feel Lost (ego).

2. Taking it to Spirit, list how you can find your way.

Wisdom

It has also been written that the thirty two paths of wisdom are encoded in our nervous system transmitting messages from our brain to all parts of our body. It also is the path in which we can reach the divine mind. This has been called the mind, body, and Spirit connection. The Divine Mind being the same as the Great Divine. We are one with the Universal God.

The thirty two paths encoded in our bodies are the ten Sefirot; know as ten vowels and twenty two letters of the Hebrew alphabet, which are said to be consonants. So our words become our world, much like God spoke the world into existence. That is how powerful words are in the Universe and how important our level of consciousness as a collective unit is to our salvation, back to Paradise. Our thoughts become feelings and our feelings become our speech.

Let me have you take a moment to scan your thoughts about yourself or your life. What are you saying? "I'm not good looking enough, rich enough, young enough or just plain not good enough." It is these very thoughts that become our feelings and then our speech into the Universe of who we are. We will want to blame others for making us feel this way, but the bottom line is no one can make us feel anything from the external; it is all an internal process with the ego thought system and the belief of separation from the One Spiritual Mind.

We are also like magnets; we tend to pull people into our space of the same ego thought system. From there we collect agreements and evidence to be right about ourselves and our conversation of: "Not being good enough."

Remember, the ego will manipulate to be a right machine. It will go so far as to subconsciously create evidence that we will find to prove it right. This is the ongoing Spiritual warfare within the mind. What mind system will we choose, ego or Spirit? If we as Spiritual Beings choose Spirit our collective consciousness will become Christ like. I believe that is what the second coming of Christ is, realizing Christ consciousness within us. Not Jesus riding up in a van holding up the peace sign saying hello gang I'm back, all of you who have been good can come with Me, and those of you that have been bad need to visit and stay in a place called Hell. How dualistic could that be?

Universal Oneness means; we are all here together for the sake of humanity. With that comes the power of the tongue in which we speak. So, if we collectively speak love into the Universe that is what we will manifest and realize that is who we really are. This is called the power of the tongue. God spoke the word of power: "Let there be light." We are one with God so we contain that very same power of speech.

What happens when we speak false negative thoughts, false negative responses happen within ourselves, and collective false negative thoughts create an unwanted cause and effect. Example: World anger, world negativity, world crisis and disasters. Creation is God manifested in our flesh. Spirit is always within us. This Spirit led by the power of thoughts that turn to feelings can have domain over all forces of the physical world. Jesus stilled the storm with the word, peace. Our word is very important; it's part of our Spirit. Where we give our word, what we say with it, how impeccable we are once we have given our commitment with it. Our being on time, doing what we said we would do once we said it. All of this adds to our Universal oneness and higher consciousness toward collective unity. It has been written that Jesus said: "I have told My people they can have what they say, but My people are saying what they have."

Process

1. What is it that you are saying about you, your life, the world and other people?

2. How does this manifest into your life?

3. List what you would like to say and manifest with the power of your word.

Chapter 3

More Roads to Rome

Can we really declare Faith and Alliance with an invisible Creator within us? Let's look at the Road called Hinduism, the study of Universal Oneness through Eastern Religion. No matter what Road we follow we're always looking for transmutation, as turning base metal into Gold (alchemy). This is what is called looking for the philosopher's stone; the Holy Grail, the keys to Solomon, Nirvana, and Brahman. No matter what path we take Universal God is always the Author of our Being. It is He who inspires us to reveal our powers through the many masks of God. The fall is present and not a past fact. We are still and always looking for paradise lost, renunciation of false belief and separation will be our new beginning of life, our paradise found at last.

What are the Masks of God? When we Pray and look to God to answer a Prayer or need, we sometimes have a perceived idea of what the answer is supposed to look like and how it will be delivered. The delivery may come in many different ways, and whoever or whatever the Mask of God is wearing at that time, especially for you. By mask I mean, different roles He plays within all of us.   The different faces in which the Spirit of God appears; the sudden skill, ability and knowledge we obtain to move forward, manifest, create and grow toward our Greater Self, which is the golden Divine Truth, that we are Spiritual Beings (God) on a human journey.

Sometimes we take a larger role for humanity. For Christians it is Jesus. For Buddhists it is Gotama. Muslins it is Mohamed. Hinduism it is Krishna. Each Religion recognizes a Divine God Head and within some Religions there can be many Incarnations of their God Head. Some try to separate Poets and Sages; but are these not all The Faces of God?

Once again, I point out Universal Oneness, one Center Point in which all comes from and returns to. Self Realization comes from knowing who we really are. We need to die an illusionary death within our misconceived minds of Dualism to start the journey back home to Oneness. Like the story of the Wizard of Oz; Dorothy wants only to go back to her home in Kansas, when all along she never left home. It

28

was only in her thoughts of unconsciousness that she believed she was in the Land of Oz, where there lived good and evil, positive and negative energies, a world of dualism. Each time a new character arrived to aid her in her search back home; it was the mask of God appearing to show her what she already had within herself. Scarecrow, the heart to Love, Tin man, a brain containing intelligence and understanding, Lion, the courage to overcome anything, and, Toto her dog, was totality; everything which was always within her. These are the archetypes of the personalities within us, the hidden God.

The story of our true identities has been told since ancient times, over and over again, but because we think ourselves to be separate from Oneness, we have failed to see the sign post on the yellow brick road that says this way to Rome,(home) paradise within us. This is only one of many stories told, some have been told through the Bible, the Bhagavad-Gita, and so many more. Even through science fiction films, poems, art, music, animation, children's stories, books and rhymes. The mask of God is always telling us our true identity for our higher purpose.

Process

1.   List the masks of God you see in your life.

2.   What masks of God do you wear?

3.   What masks of God would you like to wear?

Hinduism

My introduction into Hinduism was through the Vedanta Society, in Trabuco Canyon, California. My home church, which I will discuss in a later chapter, had a sudden change. In search for the beloved within, I received an inner message to visit a Hindu Monastery. Thanks to the internet, within minutes I found a Monastery within my local area. My husband and I proceeded to attend their lecture, and beforehand attend their meditation room. From the moment I arrived it was as if I was transported to India without the long distance travel. But more than that, I could feel the warmth and all embracing consciousness of love coming from this place. As the Swami of the day spoke, it brought tears to my eyes to hear and feel the Universal Oneness of the Godheads of all religions, being the road to Rome.

These are the things I learned; not only on that day but for the five years I attended the Monastery; that not only Hindu Deities but all Deities were acknowledged and when I entered meditation that whatever Deity I chose to meditate upon was divine, if that was the Deity I related most with. I also was given personal instruction how to meditate by requesting private time with one of the Swamis, which he gladly and generously extended. I learned the philosophy of non dualism that Brahman's absolute existence is true knowledge, and that knowledge was within us to meditate on and be one with Brahman. I instantly saw that it was the same road, except what would seem to us as an illusionary cultural difference.

As it also can seem that our ancient Scriptures are of different roads. We have the Old Testament which the Jewish call the Torah. Christians look more to the New Testament which they call the "Good News Bible." The Buddhists have Damamapada, the sacred collections of the enlightened Buddha. In Hinduism there are three books called the Scriptural Trinity-Prasthanatrayam. The three books are the Upanishads, the Brahma Sutras and the Bhagavad-Gita. There is also the Mahabharata, which seems to be of the same philosophy. The Bhagavad-Gita is the story teller, as is the Bible, of Spiritual warfare from illusionary double existence between ego and internal self, struggling to reclaim it's divinity with Brahman (God), the breath of one existence.

Our ignorance of self perception super imposes maya, an illusionary separate individual self from the world of the infinite. The Atman is the inner self, the Brahman within, or some would say the God within. The sign post of Hinduism appears different although leading to the same place. In real estate it is always location, location, location. In life it is always perception, perception, perception. That is the only way we will escape misperceived dualism of ourselves and the Universe, returning ourselves back to Brahman's tranquility of pure consciousness. Our renunciation will be the beginning of Life and our realization of ourselves as the I Am.

The Bhagavad-Gita is a Spiritual Hindu Bible, with a dialogue between four speakers in which the central characters are: King Dhristashta, Sanjaya, Arjuna and Krishna. Dhristashta is blind and the Sage Vyasa, who purportedly was the author of the Bhagavad-Gita; offers to restore his sight so he can bear witness to the battle of Kurukshetra. Dhristashta is unwilling to want to see the killing of his Kings men. He then is given psychic powers through Sanyaya, his minister and charioteer. Sanyaya describes everything he sees happening on the battlefield. Through his voice is a dialogue between Krishna and Arjuna, along with his own commentaries. Each are speaking of the battle as if it were dualism taking place, when in actuality it is a dialogue of perceiving past the Maya (illusion) of dualism, to the Brahman being Absolute All is One, playing two sides of one coin.

Life is eternal; so we need not mourn for the living or the dead, because all is infinite Spirit returning to itself and back again. It is only through Maya that we perceive both good and evil, pleasure and pain. If we look beyond the veil we could conceive consciousness of absolute reality that all is one.

The Bhagavad-Gita teaches how to be ready to deal with the illusionary battle of life, and is the most translated book, next to the Bible. I would recommend that everyone have a copy on their book shelf next to their Bible and the other great literature of their choice.

<u>Process</u>

1. List the maya (illusion) you see about yourself.

2. List the Spiritual truth thoughts you have about yourself.

Chapter 4

On The Road

I refer to plugging in to the Almighty Energy of the Universe as Oneness. I remember the movie the Matrix referred to getting unplugged from the illusionary world we perceive as real. Again, it's story telling within a sci-fi movie. Neo, the main character is the one that will wake from the walking dream via the blue pill. The film deals with artificial intelligence, sophisticated technology that becomes conscious of itself and becomes autonomous and wages wars on mankind in order to enslave them.

It is the same as in the Garden of Eden when the serpent speaks of partaking of the Fruit of Knowledge. This was advanced knowledge that God knew we were not ready to handle. For the serpent said: "God knows that when you eat of it, your eyes will be open and you will be like God, knowing of good and evil." Was this the moment of the walking dream, the split moment in time where we became conscious of ourselves, where we created artificial intelligence from God? The Bible says: "Then the eyes of them were opened and they realized they were naked." They sewed fig leaves together and made coverings for themselves, creating instant separation within the mind. Nakedness was our innocent natural way of being, but now we're saying no this individual separate person needs to cover up, because in our individual minds nakedness is sinful.

Next was fear. When they heard the sound of the Lord God, as He was walking in the garden they hid among the trees. When God called out to Adam; "Where are you?" Adam answered, I was afraid because I was naked. Next we have blame. When God asked Adam, who told you that you were naked; in other words, why the separate thoughts of nakedness. God then asked; have you eaten from the tree that I commanded you not to eat of? Adam answered, the women Eve, you put here with me, gave me some fruit from the tree and I ate it. Adam is now speaking of his oneness with Eve as separate from Himself, as he also sees himself separate from God. Eve backs him up with this illusionary separate individuality, by passing the blame onto the serpent. "The serpent deceived me and I ate it," said Eve. Final separation is banishment from the Garden of

Correction of the Ego/Spirit Mind

Eden. God said: "The man has become one of Us, knowing good and evil." God speaks of good and evil as one consciousness, with the choice, and it is certainly played out in the garden and in so many Biblical stories.

In the movie the Matrix, there is a choice of a red pill that will keep you enslaved in an illusionary world of artificial intelligence, or the blue pill that will wake you up to the reality of the dream. Whether it is fruit or pill, the message is we're dreaming ourselves away from home and looking for home in an illusionary world.

What choices do we continually make to defend our ego thought system from our Spiritual Thought System? Our Spirit Thought System needs no defending for there is nothing real to defend, but in our now separated minds we defend our nakedness, not only physically but emotionally.

This was not only our first attack on God but also on nature. For in Genesis it is written: "And the Lord God said the man has now become like one of us knowing good and evil, he must not be allowed to reach out his hand and take also from the Tree of Life and eat and live forever." So God banished man from the Garden of Eden to work from the ground of which he had taken. In our separated mind we are now separated from nature's gift of Paradise.

This was our first separated interplay with Nature that we still continuously play with our split mind, wanting Paradise here on earth but choosing ego thought system and not preserving the planet, but instead taking from it every ounce of resource it has, for us to feed the ego mind of the need for more, believing somehow we will arrive in Paradise.

God knew we were not ready for the responsibility of conscious illusionary *split mind*. Look what it cost Lucifer, the fallen angel, at the split moment of his conscious separation. Can it be that we are going in circles, suspended in a split moment in time trying to reconnect to our oneness? Time has become for us an event lived over and over again in our minds, living out of our past events and old beliefs, to create our future and completely dismissing the present. This is part of the *split mind* mentality, two thoughts occupying one space creating duality.

Have you ever noticed the peace that comes over your mind when you're in the present moment, whether it be reading a good book, getting lost in a good movie, playing or listening to music and among the most powerful, meditating, resting your mind on the stillness of the moment? Whenever we unify our thoughts from separation, we become one operating in our true essence, and also find that all events are interconnected with an inseparable phenomenon of certainty of consciousness.

We also find many possibilities though our choices of perception, a realization that we are the authors, producers and leading actors in our own divine comedy of life, that we see as separate from God. You may say, what about death? On some level that may be part of the subconscious that believes it is born to suffer and decay within its own individual script it has written for itself. The ego mind looks at death as a loss of individuality, something to fear. When we accept ourselves as pure conscious Spirits, perhaps then we can purify and transmute the decaying of the body.

This, I believe, was the healing power of Jesus; he had only one conscious thought Oneness, and if you were a believer then your consciousness crossed over to that Oneness, which brings about your true identity of mind, body and soul being one with divine purification. It is only the ego self consciousness that keeps our thoughts separated from God's thoughts.

People always ask: "Where was God when this happened, or that happened?" God is not aware of the dualism, He is only the one correction when perceived and chosen by Spiritual Beings on this human journey, to awaken to self realization. After all, roots, branches and trunk are part of the same tree.

Process

1. List when you feel separated from others.

2. List when you feel connected to others.

3. List action steps to connect with others.

Chapter 5

Pathways of Light

I was heading up a Woman's Spiritual Seminar, which was first started in my home every Tuesday evening that expanded into workshops and retreats; my Tuesday and Thursday classes were then moved to a professional office. One Saturday afternoon while doing a full day workshop, I was compelled to enter another counselor's office. There in his waiting room was a booklet that seemed to call out my name, I picked it up and knew in that instant, that I was having a serendipitous moment. I knew instantly that my consciousness had brought me here to yet another path of lightness and oneness. It was a booklet about a Spiritual College that was based on a Course in Miracles, the text books that were dictated to Dr. Helen Schucman by Jesus.

Hard to believe, but if you read the Course in Miracles you know that the information given for the correction of the *split mind* could only come from Christ Himself. It is pure in its contents of knowing, reminding us that we are part of the Sonship that is part of the Oneness with God; we are like droplets from the ocean, two aspects of one in the same. The Course teaches about the ego thought system, how to recognize itself and the illusionary false thinking that has made an unreal world real to the mind.

What the Course emphases is that what we need is a correction of our thoughts and we can find that inner wisdom by taking the hand of a new Teacher, Jesus Christ, the Christ within us. Our mind is separated by two thought systems, ego and Spirit. Ego was made up at the split moment in time by a tiny mad idea, where the Son of Man forgot to laugh.

My thoughts are that whatever becomes conscious of itself becomes a *split mind*, like a child who becomes conscious of itself at about the age of two. They no longer feel that they are at one with the caretaker. Every thought becomes a feeling, so thoughts of separation now become feelings of separation. Have you ever had that empty feeling within you, where you thought something or someone else outside of you could fix it? That perfect partner or friendship, or the new house you always wanted, only to find out after the excitement of getting it, you were soon onto the next search for happiness.

When we see accomplishments someone makes and we learn how horribly sad they were or are, or when we read about their suicide or drug abuse we realize it is never the external thing that brings us extended happiness, but it is the internal thoughts of happiness that create the feelings of contentment, and if we want to hang on and prolong these thoughts it will be an exercise in correction between wrong and right mind thinking.

I believe our Soul is within our body, the part of God that was given to us. When we left the Garden of Eden we took this Soul with us. What also followed us out was the Trinity; Father, Son and Holy Spirit, which activates the Soul's knowingness of who we really are. You may have heard the phrase, "Deep down in your Soul, what do you know that you know?" When activated with right mindedness you have the Holy Trinity within you. By believing in the fall of mankind we create separation of guilt, fear and sin, that we have killed off God and that part of ourselves is always longing for wholeness. It is only the insane thinking of the ego mind that will look outside itself for wholeness.

Whether we think the Biblical account of Eden is real or not we may never know. For what is real and what is made up outside of the Holy Spirit? We make it all up to fit inside a form of a world made up of separation and specialness. Within the Oneness of God there is just Creation. The Course says: "You cannot walk the world apart from God, because you cannot be without Him. He is what your life is, where you are He is, there is one life, that life you shall share with Him. Nothing can be apart from Him and live."

The Course in Miracles message is clear; teach only love which is forgiveness, for that is what you are. The Bible is also the message of love, choosing the wrong mind or the right mind. It's just written in a different context for the Holy Spirit within us to perceive. From this we can come to understand that both Paradise and the fall are pieces of the same mystery, and both are essential to the human condition of mastering our Spiritual Mind.

Process

1. In what areas do you desire to master your mind?

2. What action steps do you need to take?

3. What have been and what will be the positive consequences?

Chapter 6

Road to Self Spiritual Awakening

One of the most important tools I have learned as an Ordained Ministerial Counselor, through Pathways of Light Spiritual College is a process called Self Awakening Spiritual Counseling. It is a deeply guided meditation facilitated through Spiritual Counseling. It guides you into a visual meditation by first looking at what is called a thought cluster. A thought cluster is a thought within the subconscious mind that is causing a dis-ease which leads to a feeling of discomfort. Remember, every thought becomes a feeling.

When we are unaware of these thought clusters we react in ways in which we find undesirable, or as if it has control over us instead of us having control over it. When we are guided through visual meditation into the subconscious mind we can then shut down the mind chatter and look at the unconscious thought cluster that is causing the chaos. As the doors to our higher wisdom are open we gain knowledge of the fear, tension and worry surrounding our thought cluster, but by examining it through our higher wisdom within we can heal our perception of the thought cluster, and break through self created barriers that will then free up our inner channels of communication, allowing us to go into inner resources of more creative, positive, empowering perceptions of our thoughts and feelings. This will happen when *ego thought system* is put aside and Inner Spirit is allowed to guide us. The same Spirit we think as above us is within us. "As so above as below."

There is a phrase called Tabula Raza, which is a Latin term meaning: clean slate. The term Tabula Raza stems from ancient Greece, where in 400 BC the philosopher Aristotle stated: "The mind is a clean tablet upon which experience writes." So, how we perceive our experiences is very important whether negative or positive, it is inscribed on our tablet (the mind). Unless we *clean slate* muddled misinformation from false perceptions of the mind it will become overloaded with negativity. So when you're attempting to have positive thoughts, the Law of Physics takes hold that two thoughts can not occupy the same space at the same time, for one will cancel out the other. Then what you have is a quandary within your own mind, where you can not see clearly and are in indecision as to what your thoughts, which turn into feelings, are. Here is an example: "I can't do this." " I'm not smart enough." "I'll never get it done." (negative thoughts) Or: "I am smart enough." I will figure this out." "I will do this," (positive thoughts). By choosing the positive thoughts you then end the mind's quandary, leading you into positive actions.

God desires us to master our mind for the highest good, not only for ourselves but for humanity. The Bible is filled with stories of quandaries within the human mind in which positive right mind thinking was needed for mankind's salvation. The crucifixion was to demonstrate the resurrection; I believe Jesus rose again to show us He never really died, that it was all within the collective consensus reality of the ego, believing in a dualistic God that would allow his Son to be crucified by man. Jesus may have left the physical form He took on, but He remains in all of us. When we just work at getting through the negative perceptions of the ego thought system we can experience the Christ Consciousness that is our heritage.

Process

1. List the muddled information you have on the tablet of your mind.

2. What negative opinions do you have about your muddled information?

3. What positive facts do you have about your muddled information?

4. Using the process of tabular Raza (clean slating) utilize the facts to clear the negative perceptions.

Meditation

There are so many roads that can lead us on to the right path if we allow our Inner Teacher to teach us one way, which is the right minded thinking of Oneness.

Meditation is a very high form of higher consciousness and whether you use a Spiritual Counselor or meditate alone, either with a CD, or in a group it is a very powerful tool for this classroom of life in which we made up to learn who and what we really are. We simply need to seek and find the Spiritual Counselor within us that will deepen and awaken our true purpose in God's Divine Plan for us, not our plans for Him.

As written in Psalms 49:3: "My mouth shall speak wisdom and meditation of my heart shall give me understanding." Meditation is designed to overcome the false reality of a *split mind*. Remember that we were given the *Breath of God*. What would have us believe that we should not use it as a fine musical instrument for inner peace? By closing our eyes, calming our breath flowing with it mindfully, we can find a center within ourselves that is a direct connection to God. There was a time when such an idea could have been considered blasphemy. How wonderful it is to have the freedom in this time and space to help teach the correction of the mistaken identity of the *split mind*. Bible stories can perhaps be better understood from a meditated state. When it speaks of Jacob wrestling with God, it is not God becoming human, it is Jacob experiencing himself as a Spiritual being while meditating, and continuing with his Spiritual new insight as to his true identity, Israel a leader of a Nation. How many of us can benefit through meditative insights to our greater selves and understanding our purpose for our lives?

Refer to Chapter 16, "How to use the Meditations," Page 166.
Feel free to use the meditations in Chapter 16 page 166 at this time.

"*You must be the change you wish to see in the World.*"
Mahatma Gandhi

Process

1. List your meditation practices. How often and where?

2. If you don't have a meditation practice, start one.

3. Record your meditation results weekly.

On Prayer

Prayer is an open communication through your thoughts into a higher realm of consciousness that is within you. It puts you in direct communication with the Almighty Universal Energy Source, God. It quiets down the human being that is in form and allows the Spiritual being to channel in, like radio waves, to receive messages of healing and new perceptions. When we are in alignment with our thoughts of the power within us it causes a Universal effect to create and manifest what our true intention, hopes, dreams and aspirations are.

Some people ask why my prayers haven't been answered. That's when it's time to look within the ego thought system and see what can be blocking your reception. There may be a subconscious thought that overrides the energy waves, such as: "I'm undeserving;" caused by a shadow aspect of the ego's collective shadow personalities, which are inherit in all of us. Carl Jung was one of the first to modernize Plato's theory of personality archetypes, which live in our collective unconscious mind. Each archetype has a shadow dimension hidden within us.

We can be a hero or a victim. We can act like a child or an adult, just to name a few of what would seem like dual parts of a personality, when in reality it is all part of the same mind system. It is again that free choice of choosing from one of the same. Jesus taught that when we pray to not babble on and on. For the Lord God already knows what our needs are.

He taught the Lord's Prayer, as an example of how we can pray.

"Our Father Who Art in Heaven
Hallow be Thy Name, Thy Kingdom Come
Thy Will be done, on Earth as It
is in Heaven. Give us this Day
Our daily Bread and Forgive
Us Our Trespasses as
We Forgive those Who Trespass Against
Us, and Lead Us not into Temptation, but Deliver us From Evil.
For Thou Is the Kingdom and the
Power and the Glory Forever."

All we need to do is affirm and align ourselves with the *Almighty Spirit* that is within us on earth. Our daily bread is to learn the correction and master the mind, to know that we have all that we want and all that we need already within us. Forgiveness plays a great part of the mastering of the mind, for power and glory is all there really is in the non-dualistic thought system of oneness. Wouldn't deliverance of evil be the deliverance of ego?

Process

1. List your prayer practice, when and where.

2. What results are you receiving from your prayers?

3. Make a list of prayer requests and why.

4. Check them off as they are manifested.

On Chanting

We sometimes associate chanting with something that takes place in monasteries, for monks, nuns, shamans, etc. Chanting is one more road to quieting the mind chatter long enough to tap into a consciousness of your true Spiritual identity, letting go of the world's daily false illusion and experiencing yourself as whole and complete. Again, whether you chant with a group, a CD, or alone you can benefit greatly.

While I was away at Pathways of Light Spiritual College, a group of us used drums, flutes and tambourines and began an esoteric musical vibration of chanting on the banks of Lake Michigan. At another time in a more remote farm like atmosphere with a bonfire and dancing, it became a very heightened experience under the Wisconsin moon. This was not the first or the last time I had experienced higher states of Spiritual consciousness while chanting, but it was among my most memorable times.

If we think about it we have always chanted in one form or another; while doing Hail Mary's, singing in a church, monastery or temple. Even as children reciting nursery songs, we were chanting. Even chanting alone is a powerful tool for lifting one's spirit, whether it's an ancient chant of your chosen Spiritual path or one that you made up using the various names of God, as divine Spirit within to help connect and master mind, body and soul to oneness. Remember, what you practice you get good at. Keep in mind your breathing and your intention of love for yourself and humanity; always affirming that all is one.

Process

Chant your favorite song or make up one.

Here is my favorite chant. "Om Namaha Shivaya," which has been written to be translated as: "I honor the Divine within".

Om na-ma Shi – va, Om na-ma Shi –va, Om na-ma Shi –va, Shi –va om na – ma.

Start your chanting for 5 minutes, working toward extended periods of time.

When completed write down your experiences.

Tongues

Tongues are a universal language that breaks all barriers of illusionary separation from the *God Head*. Every culture has a language that prays, meditates and speaks in that language, for the most part. When we speak in tongues it is a non stop rapid chanting of words being meditated on. We need not think what the words are, we only need to experience the higher consciousness of Spirit that we desire to connect with, the Spirit that is within us that needs to correct and connect our *split mind* to Oneness.

The Bible speaks about the Day of Pentecost in which the apostles began to speak in other tongues as the Spirit enabled them, and that each person present was able to hear them in their own native language. Prior to that they saw tongues of fire that seemed to separate and rest on each of them, bringing a unity of language that could be understood by all. One message and one thought was to be heard the language of God. If you practice rapid speaking with that one thought in mind you will be surprised to hear what you will sound like as you may experience familiar languages from your memory cells taking you to a higher Universal consciousness.

Process

1. Practice alone in a quiet place, opening your mouth to rapid speaking without thinking what is coming out and experience your language of tongues.

2. Write down your experiences.

Visualization

Visualization is a technique of calling forth your desires, seeing it in an imaginary way in your mind, in order to source the energy of the God within to manifest what you want to accomplish in your life path. As part of the great energy field we have access to direct our positive energy and what would be a magnetic force of bringing forth those things that are not. By simply seeing them through our thought system we begin an alignment of manifestation.

In our false illusionary mind we can also create chaos with dualistic thoughts of opposites. In visualization it is very important to remember the *One Almighty Energy Force* as being singular. How does it work? Much like other roads to Rome keeping in mind forgiveness and love as being one and that we are made in the eyes of the Creator; we are designed to create greatness for humanity. Each step we take is a giant step for humanity, when we look at past, present and future being all the same moment in time in the correction of the *split mind*.

When we use clear mental pictures in our mind they become thoughts and feelings with divine focus and positive creative actions of energy, we can be like an artist painting on a blank canvas much the way God did when He created the heavens and the earth to be a singular Idea. Each time God created He acknowledged His accomplishments by declaring this is good, that same acknowledgement is inherently ours to tap into.

As co-creators we can start with a mental picture of what we desire for the highest good, not only for ourselves but for the universe. We then utilize our Spiritual thought system to breath, meditate, pray, affirm and write down positive action steps to be followed for the mastery of the correct creative mind. This can be done alone, with a CD or in a group.

When I teach these skills I also utilize what is called goal mapping, using magazines, scissors and glues sticks. A goal map creates a material visualization that can be created on the following pages to help remind the unconscious mind what the conscious mind desires to live into, which would be super consciousness of divine collective creation. Whether it is world peace, good health, Spiritual awareness of our life's purpose or even the job, car, house we want to manifest while we are in this world but not of this World, will take us to a higher consciousness of our creative power.

Process

Create a Goal Map

Goal Map

Affirmations

Affirmations are to make firm what you have chosen; to follow that choice with actions. It's to clearly state a declaration as if it has already happened, to stand in the belief of its existence; it is the key that opens all other doors of positive thoughts and feelings. When we affirm to think about the peace we want through our Spiritual thought system that is what we are attracting. When we look to the ego mind, we attract ego minded thoughts. Whether it is what we want to experience or what we must not experience we still attract that which is of the ego and therefore a false identity in a fictitious world of illusion.

We personalize how other people are acting or what they are saying, we write their acts into our script to help us play out our hidden motives of finding evidence that we are separate individual beings. When we watch a television program we acknowledge it was only a television program. Not so with life, we tend to think our television program goes on and on with the same script, never realizing it can be changed at any time when we no longer affirm it as true. If you don't like your story you have the power to change the thoughts that created it, even if it's a tragic story. We need to ask ourselves, what we can learn, what can we teach or help others to learn. Where is it we can go for healing outside the form of what we think our Identity is? The answer is nothing exists outside of us, we make up our existence.

As a Spiritual Counselor I have helped many people learn the art of affirmations by first getting them very clear on what they want, then affirming it not only by saying it but also by writing it down, being very specific about the details. I have even had them write a letter to themselves dating it a year in advance, acting as if it has already happened. They usually send a copy to someone who can really champion their higher good to help align with them, for where two or more are gathered miracles happen. You can write the name of that person or persons and then what you have affirmed and accomplished within that year so that each day you step into the future you have co-created with the universal Spiritual thought system.

Process

1. Make a list of positive affirmations.

2. Turn your affirmations into a one year letter form using the next page .

3. Make a copy and send it to a trusted person who will champion and align with you.

<u>One Year Letter</u>

Tithing

In the Bible, it is written in Malachi 3:10 "Bring the whole tithe into the storehouse, that there may be food in my house." "Test me in this," says the Lord Almighty, "and see if I will not throw open floodgates of Heaven and pour out so much blessings that you will not have enough room for it. I will cast their fruit," says the Lord Almighty, "then all nations will call you blessed, for yours will be a delightful land," says the Lord Almighty.

Tithing is a way to give back to the universe. It is energy that comes your way and flows back as easy as it came, it ties to the Universal Law of giving and receiving. For when we give we receive, maybe not at the exact same moment but somewhere along the line it comes back, even if it's the moment of joy of giving in its self.

The idea is to let go and let God. You will know where to tithe because it just feels right. For some it will be their church, temple, or monastery, for others charity, it is wherever God's work is being done, or a God given need is present. Some people are amazed at the power of tithing, it is hard for them to get started, but once they experience the Universal Law of God, they know there's something beyond their understanding and written words: "In God we trust" on our currency. Why do I address tithing, because it's all part of the Spiritual giving and receiving of oneness. Tithing stands for one tenth; is one tenth of one hundred too much to give back to oneness?

Process

1. Where do you tithe or would like to tithe?

2. If it is economically difficult, what could you give?

Chapter 7

Our Dreams Can Help Our Journey Home

Looking again at the Bible, whether we believe it or not it is a legacy left for us to decode, unscramble like a jigsaw puzzle, or take it word for word. Angels would appear through dreams and visions. It was while Adam was sleeping that God created Eve. When God rested on the seventh day, did that help dream us into existence?

We are told of the story of Joseph and his gift of dream interpretation. He is able to interpret the Pharaoh's dreams as being one and the same. When Pharaoh dreams of seeing seven heads of grain full and good, growing on a single stalk, after that seven other heads sprout withered and thin swallowing up the seven good heads. Prior to that in his dream he saw seven fat cows that were eaten up by seven lean ugly cows. Joseph's interpretation was that God revealed to Pharaoh in two forms what he must do for the cause of Egypt's salvation. The interpretation meant seven years of abundance followed by seven years of famine that would be experienced as one and the same by storing a fifth of the harvest during the abundance as a reserve for the seven years of famine. What would it be like if we balanced our thoughts this way, storing our Spiritual thoughts as a reserve for our negative thoughts, for the salvation of our right mind thinking?

Dreams hold the key to the solutions we are seeking, held in the subconscious mind. They come to us in an abstract way much as the Bible is for some of us. Looking to understand our dreams in order to better understand life's purpose is very powerful. They can give us guidance, foretell of a future event or unscramble what is going on in the subconscious mind.

Most of us were not brought up being asked the question, what did you dream last night and let's look at what it may mean. Some cultures do practice dream interpretation from generation to generation.

Correction of the Ego/Spirit Mind

This was not the case for me. I was told I had a vivid imagination or it was nothing more than a nightmare. The more the dream would become like a vivid experience for me, or things throughout the day would happen and I would remember I dreamed it, made me more aware of the power of dreams. As I matured I studied and learned a great deal about dreams, and how to program myself to remember them. I learned to keep a dream Journal next to my bed and upon awaking from a dream I would write it down right away with any and all details. Next, was learning to ask myself what each detail personally meant to me and what I associated it with? This is not always easy as dreams can be so abstract at times, but with the knowledge that it is just a symbol of what the subconscious mind has stored, helps to break it down to one's own association.

There are many books that help out with symbolism, but one's own personal symbolism can be very powerful in the knowingness of the subconscious mind. Only you know what personal meaning you perceive things as. By breaking your dreams down you can get closer to your truth of the ego mind that sometimes will use nightmares to get our attention, or what we perceive as nightmares. Once you are able to identify that you are dreaming, and that usually happens when the ridiculous shows up. The moment you can say, this is a nightmare you can then turn around and chase the three hundred foot tall monster away, knowing that you are really facing your own three hundred foot ego mind monster, and confronting yourself and asking what do I want to know about myself or my life.

Most dreams are aspects of our shadow side coming to the surface in order to deliver a message. Having a devoted listener for dream interpretation is important. I believe what God desired Pharaoh to know was aided by Joseph, two working as one for the salvation God intended for Egypt, all working as one.

Our dreams are working as divine Spiritual messages helping to give us problem solving inspiration in any and all areas of our life. To a composer a symphony, to an inventor a problem solved. For me, it was writing this book among other things. There it was one night in my dream, a library with a book called, The Correction of the Ego/Spirit Mind. I knew instantly that was the name of the book I was supposed to write. Before that I had no idea I would be writing a book, after that all the dreams that followed were like Spirit guides working with me.

If I were moving along they were more gentle and loving in my dreams. If I was procrastinating there were dreams of doors, keys, hallways, stairs and someone always getting on my case for not using the keys, unlocking the door, walking through the hall and up the stairs. Dreams can come in series with the same symbolism, like flying, or water or a mountain; whatever it is the subconscious mind uses as knowledge that the conscious mind is unaware of.

Why do I write about dreams; because they too are signposts leading us to the road to Rome. It is powerful to our personal understanding of life, when we read these signposts as omens, prophesies and messages for our true Spiritual oneness. It's much like our walking dream. Sometimes we need to weed through the nonsense to get to Spiritual truth of who we are.

Worry and repression are some of the ego's illusionary tricks playing on what we think are our reality, creating a subconscious pile on within our psyche that re-enacts them in the sleeping dream state, sometimes working on more than one subconscious thought at a time. That's why they can seem so odd.

If we think about it, isn't that what we're experiencing in our walking dream. How many of us are fully present to the moment? Don't we have abstract ideas flowing to the surface of our mind? Like when someone is talking and your mind is already dreaming up what it wants to say in response, I call that "a preconceived listening." That's where you are on automatic pilot and not in the actual moment of what the other person is saying or doing, along with all the other activities going on around you.

In our sleeping dream we are actually more conscious as observers to the subconscious mind of what's actually going on, rather than a "preconceived listening" of our perception of what's going on. There's no mistake that God keeps providing ways for us to make it home. Sigmund Freud described dreams as "the royal road to the unconscious."

Process

Use the blank pages and begin to record your dreams upon awakening. Look at every detail and ask the question: "What association do I have with this?" Write down your answers and you will begin to unravel what is going on in your sub-conscious mind. You can also share your dream with a trusted person and listen to their dream asking the question: "What do you associate that with," thereby helping them to come up with their conclusions. Be open to each other's insights; just be aware that your most important insight is your perception of your inner truth based on your dream.

Dream Journal

<u>Dream Journal</u>

Dream Journal

<u>Dream Journal</u>

Chapter 8

The Road to Heaven

The Bible starts with Genesis and tells of the Garden of Eden. I see it as a metaphoric story of the birth of the human ego mind, choosing outside of its true spiritual contents, believing itself to be a form with external life outside of itself and God, making itself an illusionary garden of its own identity, a garden outside the pillar of flames of the one true Eden.

We believe ourselves undeserving of our union with God and falsely perceive ourselves through the ego mind of thought and separation from one another, when in Spiritual reality we are all seeds in a garden of potentiality, the same garden we started in before we lost Paradise in our illusionary mind. We sometimes fight for who will be the award winning flower in the garden, not realizing a flower is a flower. Some are different colors, sizes and height but they are still flowers that bloom together or at different times in order to orchestrate the garden of life.

I am reminded of Alice's Adventures in Wonderland with the golden key, wanting to go through the little door and down the long hallway into the garden, believing nothing is impossible. That is what we have, a golden key to what seems like a little door and a long walk down a long hallway to the garden of our true essence. Jesus said: "It is easier for a camel to go through the eye of a needle, then a rich man to enter the Kingdom of God." Scott Peck's book calls it the road less traveled. I call it the road that takes you longer to get there, but we are all designed in the Eyes of the Creator to get there; we just need to continuously unite our mind to meet there. Like the mushroom in Alice's Adventures in Wonderland, one side will make you smaller the other side will make you larger, but it is still the same mushroom.

I have been asked, how does a person stay in the present moment? In my husband's book, he writes about a method he was taught, where at the moment of becoming conscious of not being in the present moment by worrying about what's next or what you haven't done, what someone else will say, or what they said in the past; you the being at that point stops the mental dialogue, changes it to engage in the present dialogue then starts a conscious creation to what the moment is, identifying with ego mind thinking or spiritual mind thinking. Your spiritual thoughts are enlightening. Your ego minded thoughts are burdening. Both appear as opposites to the illusionary thought process we have invented for the ego mind to survive.

It's not until we come to realize we have a choice as to what we make up as truth to ourselves that we can practice it, in order to get good at being fully conscious of the moment that is. We are always in past or future thinking, rarely in the present that is. In the Divine Comedy, by Dante Alighieri, he writes about humans being at the center of the earth and that we were to be perfect creations between heaven and hell replacing the fallen angels and that in the early life we were to be in perfect unity and consciousness with God.

After the fall in the Garden of Eden we forfeited our earthly perfection that would move us up to the higher realms of heaven. It is my thought that if the mind allows itself to choose ego thought system it will remain in a Purgatorial state, fearing hell and not allowing Spiritual consciousness to the state of heaven. We haven't the real concept of dualism verses oneness as yet but as we move more to a collective consciousness we will reach higher realms of awareness toward oneness.

We are not able to bring God to us but we are able to reach God though inner manifestation that is our true heritage. We can be like magicians if we allow our right mind thinking to take hold of whatever situation we are dealing with. There is nothing outside of who you are.

If you were to stare into a mirror and really take in your perception of yourself you would see only a reflection of your made up self and any thoughts that are being manufactured in your mind are coming from an idea, either a Spiritual one or an ego minded one. You can always identify it by how the thoughts effect your emotions. If you feel sad and not enough it's ego, if you feel happy and more than enough it's Spirit. Spirit will always lead you to positive emotions generated from Spiritual thought system that masters our observation which becomes our behavior of mastery of the mind that God desires us to have. This can also change the physical effect we have with our bodies. We see our bodies as a separate identity of its own, not realizing we have made our body image within our mind.

What we put our thoughts on, whether we want it or not, is still putting our thoughts on something. There's a little song I love that says: "Our thoughts are prayers and we are always praying. To be aware of what we're saying, to hold a higher consciousness, a place of peacefulness." When sickness, guilt and fear are no longer in the mind we will experience Heaven. We may not be able to bring heaven here but we can at least follow the path toward heaven.

It is written that Abraham Lincoln once said:

"Most folks are about as happy as they make up their mind to be."

Process

1. What have you been putting your thoughts on that are not your desired outcome?

2. How can you turn these thoughts into your desired outcome?

3. What action steps do you need to take for your desired outcome?

Encountering the Meter Reader

Path to the Subconscious Mind

I now came to understand that there was a Spiritual mind and an ego mind, but what was it that exactly fed the ego mind and how could one get a deeper awareness of it. The road was right in front of me, my friend and business partner had been trained for more than a decade to utilize what is called a Clarity Bio Feedback Meter. It was developed in the 1890's. Swiss physiologist Carl Jung spoke and wrote of the method of using a device with hand held electrodes connected to a measuring instrument, something that would be like one component of three of a polygraph (lie detector) test that could read galvanic skin response. Once used with the right list of questions could stimulate the repressed thoughts held within the sub-conscious mind, thereby freeing them up to come to the surface of full realization and release.

We sometimes are completely unaware of what is causing us pain from the past. We simply continue to carry on that pain in our memory cells, or as Eckhart Tolle wrote in "A New Earth," the pain body. Studies continued throughout the early 1900's describing the cell memory as an engram, coined by Alfred Korzybski. An engram is something that has taken place within the Ego thought system of survival, like a snap shot in the mind, being unaware that the snap shot has even been taken, and then living out a script based on the unawareness. Awareness of this modality continues to grow with different kinds of bio feedback meters, and subjective questions aimed at stimulating the subconscious mind.

L. Ron Hubbard wrote about the engram of the mind in his book, "Dianetics," written in the 1950's. Volney Mathieson, an American researcher who worked with the polygraph, presented his invention of a modern sophisticated version of the galvanic skin response meter to L. Ron Hubbard, who then created his own version now called the E meter.

I am not affiliated with Scientology. I am an independent Spiritual teacher, always looking for ways of connection and oneness.

Correction of the Ego/Spirit Mind

My training was extensive through a different schooling and my advancement and ongoing knowledge is continuous. I have been working as a Certified Processor for Clearing, since the year 2000.

It never ceases to amaze me how our stories of the ego thought system drives us into the same dissatisfying behavior over and over again, until we are able to observe it and allow Holy Spirit to help us lay it down, in order to get to the cause within, that will get us to the accumulated effects of *split mind* thinking. As a "Course in Miracles" says: "Projection makes perception." Our goal is to correct our projection to identify with the right perception.

When I work with clients it is always so rewarding to help them identify for themselves what they perceive and why they perceive it, along with the consequences they are generating. The deeper we go into their earlier similar events we identify the first initial shock that took place that became the emotional thought of pain, that they then live into.

The good news is we do not need to stay stuck in our stories. As we become aware of the pain we start to blow down the energy field around it, and we are able to identify it as: "Oh there it is, that feeling of loneliness," or any other negative feelings that may be discovered. The mind now has a chance to choose what it must not experience, bypassing the circuits of loneliness etc., into a new conversation of contentment and peace.

I find that processing the subconscious mind with a bio-feedback meter is not only useful because of the commands that take you straight to the source of the subconscious thoughts and allows you to replay them as an observer, but it also allows you to down load your responses to those thoughts and reload them with new ones. Once you can identify that the cheese down that old tunnel doesn't taste so good you will be more prompt to go up the new tunnel you have created with Spiritual consciousness. What bio-feedback does is to help take the subconscious thoughts and helps to make them conscious, choosing a different way of seeing yourself and then seeing the world in a different way, bringing us back to universal knowledge of wholeness and to be present to the moment.

Some of us just need to be heard, with proper instructional methods and to have a committed listener who is holding a place of peace for us. You may not be working with a person trained in bio-feedback with a meter, but you can ask yourself the following questions for self processing your mind of illusionary thoughts from the past in order to bring them to the present and choose a conscious decision for the future.

<u>Sample Commands for Clarity</u>

Pick an item you are struggling with.

1. What remembrance do you have of that?

2. Did something like that happen before, and what did you experience?

3. Go to the first time you remember that occurring.

4. What did you make up about that?

5. From that time on what has been your level of consciousness?

6. From where could you create a higher level of Spiritual consciousness?

Correction of the Ego/Spirit Mind

Again, I say; this is not a book on bio-feedback or any other subject in itself. It is an overview of the different modalities that are available to us and acknowledging that it is all an inside job of love, forgiveness and awareness of our Spiritual wholeness.

We are all seeking the truth of who and what we are. We may get sidetracked from time to time but knowing where to ask, knock and open doors in our mind will bring us back to our Center.

Ask and it will be given to you, seek and you will find, knock and the door will be opened to you.

Matthew 7:7

Chapter 9

The Road to Consciousness

Why me? Why have I chosen to write this book? Those are the questions I ask myself. The answer always comes back the same; "Because God wants you to, your whole life path has been leading up to this." Every person along the way, each book, course and Spiritual learning, and yes tragedy has built upon this book. I am writing about my Spiritual quest but I have not yet shared my unconscious existence, when I wasn't aware that there was an ego thought system running my life and who I thought I was. I didn't realize the sad pitiful drama I created for myself, was a one woman show with actors written in to help me play my part. I had to hit the lowest of my B movie script to realize there had to be something more to life.

How did this come about? Well, here it is. One day at thirty three years of age I woke up in a jail cell trying to focus on the night before, what happened, why am I here wearing an orange jumpsuit that workers on the side of the freeway wear. Where was the pink robe I remember wearing, what seemed like a few hours ago. What time is it and why am I here?

As I laid there I began to slowly remember bits and pieces as the story started to unfold. I'm at home wearing a pink robe; my daughters are staying the night with friends. There is an angry abusive script being played out between my now ex-husband and myself. On and on it goes. The last words I remember him saying were: "You are nothing, you will never be anything, I want out." After being boxed between the ears the night before, everything went black. I could see my actions, it was as if I was having an out of body experience, as I picked up steak knives and repeatedly yelled out: "I'll give you out!" I must have had an unfamiliar look on my face because he began to run out the door and down the street. There was that pink robe open wide like a cape with only panties and a bra underneath and no slippers on. I began to run after him throwing each steak knife unconsciously toward his back, never making a hit. (Thank you God)

Tired and feeling out of sorts with what felt like uncontrollable anxiety I walked home, poured a drink and fell asleep on the couch. The next thing I remember is being awakened by a knock on the door. As I opened the door my ex-husband and two police officers walked into my home and found a steak knife I had brought back. The police immediately hand cuffed me, put me under arrest and escorted me to the backseat of their police car. All of this is going on as if I'm seeing it as an out of body experience.

We have heard the story where a person has lifted a car to free their child from beneath it. It is called adenosine triphosphate (ATP), a chemical from the brain released into the muscles that cause what some call elephant strength or super human survival strength. That was part of the unaware nervous breakdown I was experiencing. Till this day I don't know how I did it but I was able to escape from the handcuffs, open the back door of the police car and head back to my front door. Before I could reach my door I was tackled by the two policemen. With ATP it took both of them to keep me down and controlled. I had completely lost it, no consciousness no control.

Now I was lying in a top bunk still wondering where that pink robe was. Till this day I wonder what happened to it; the lost moment of the robe to the orange jumpsuit has always remained a blank to me. As the ego does it works on our worse fears and vulnerabilities. I was sick and sinful and I deserved to die for this. As I listened to the negative mind chatter I began to unravel the sleeping blanket given to me. I looked up and saw a vent and began to hook the unraveled sleeping blanket through it to create a noose to hang myself. The ego voice inside my mind was telling me to hang myself because my life was over and I wasn't fit to be a mother after this. That's when God's Universal Energy swept into my life. I was being watched on a monitor and my suicide attempt was stopped. I was then taken to another jail and put in a psychiatric cell, until someone could come and evaluate the situation and circumstance.

That's when I started seeing the mask of God. The first was a lovely woman evaluator working for my insurance company. She gave me the love and kindness I so needed at the moment. Her faith in me had me start to realize I was more than I thought I was at that time.

The next day I spent handcuffed to what looked like a chain gang, sitting in a court room waiting for the judge to address my case. He was the second mask of God. He took one look at me and knew I was like a fish out of water and only held me responsible for getting the help I needed.

I can't remember clearly if it was that day or the next day that I was released to the hospital. It is still all foggy to me how many days I spent in jail, what I ate and if I ate. I know I didn't use the open toilet sitting in the cell. I only remember I was in a deep sleep most of the time.

After that came the third mask of God, introduction to my psychiatrist. He assured me I had only suffered a small breakdown and through counseling, everything would work out, and that my ex-husband had dropped charges against me and had arranged through our insurance for a pack team and an ambulance to take me from the jail to College Hospital for treatment. My ego identity was now telling me I was a nut case and I was slowly and unconsciously playing out that part.

Then the forth mask of God appeared, it was a wonderful Japanese co-worker who always spoke to me about the power of knowing God. When he arrived to visit me he brought with him a Bible, a nightgown and slippers. Yes, I was still wearing the orange jumpsuit.

That night I began to read scripture after scripture, not really understanding what I was reading but having a sense of something far greater within me, a sudden consciousness of something collectively going on around me. As I looked around at all the collective unhappiness, depression and suicide attempts it hit me all at once we are making all this up, we are all in a story that our ego identity has manufactured to make it real and that we manifest what we need to keep the story going.

With my insurance running out and my psychiatrist giving the ok, it was time for me to leave, but where would I go. I knew full well if I went back home my sorry story would continue to play out. My ex-husband was not transformed. My psychiatrist tried to have him and I seek couples counseling, which my ex-husband was not an opening for.

Then my fifth mask of God showed up, who was not only a Life/Success Coach but also had gone through such programs as Forum, Life Spring and also took transformation training to Russia. He introduced me to these trainings. They provided me with more tools for inner wisdom. As I continued my road to Rome I eventually married my fifth mask of God, and together we have built a successful Spiritual coaching practice, called Power Technology.

Process

1. What story have you acted out about yourself?

2. What new positive story can you produce for yourself?

3. Who has shown up as the mask of God in your life?

The Road to Enlightenment

My husband and I felt that a Spiritual family such as a Church was something that would enhance our Spiritual journey. Living in South Orange County, we were very fortunate to live near San Juan Capistrano Church located on a lovely ranch. Not being involved in church for a very long time it was a new experience for me, to actually become a church member and to enjoy a church family. The sermons were always very uplifting, combined with the positive thinking method of Spirituality. I enjoyed my involvement with what was then called Balance for Life. It gave me the opportunity to contribute to others by becoming a small group leader and becoming a crisis counselor at the Crystal Cathedral Church, which was another way of my contribution to others.

Whenever we are in service to others we are contributing to all of humanity. That is why it is also necessary to allow others to contribute to us. This modality was Christianity. The teachings at the church fit us very well; we were always learning the *Good News*, intertwined with positive thinking for today's world. I found it with less dogma and light and easy. I even joined the women's Bible study group. The ranch that the church was on, provided a place for my husband and I to facilitate Spiritual Ropes Courses.

I write of these experiences because life is ever changing and we are ever changing. A thought can split from one moment to another moment, going into automatic ideas, habits and perceptions, turning into projections of the world. If we are rigid and consumed with dogma we lose out on the chance for growth. It's when we step out of the box and explore the many paths to Rome that are available to us that we can experience the notes that make the music that are of the same musical scale.

Our Minister eventually moved on. I felt for awhile that my Spiritual world was turned upside down, as the new minister, no fault on his part, just didn't resonate with my personal growth and journey. I find it very important to know when it is time to encounter new knowledge for inner wisdom, to be open to what's possible. Learning and teaching Spiritual knowledge is a lifetime commitment, like exercising. We just don't exercise for a couple of years, and then say, "that's done" and still expect to stay fit.

Process

1. Where do you receive Spiritual Enlightenment?

2. Where else could you receive Spiritual Enlightenment?

Our Kingdom is within us

We can build our Spiritual peace within the temple of our mind. When we train our Spiritual mind to rely on the Spiritual side of thinking we create joy, love and enthusiasm from within that then radiates outward to all we come in contact with. Teaching by actions is the most powerful. When asked, why doesn't that bother you, how can you be so calm about that, is when you can walk the walk that matches your talk. To label something negative, like: "I'm mad, worried or sad," is to name it. When you name it, what you've named is something real to the illusionary mind, and you will look for all the evidence to try proving it is real. By allowing the thought to rise to the surface and turning it over to the Holy Spirit, we can better learn to lay it down and continue our mind training toward Spiritual conscientiousness of peace, forgiveness and love.

The doctrine of Christianity is that through Christ we have the Counselor within us, called the Holy Spirit. There is also a belief in the Trinity; Father, Son and Holy Spirit. Father who created us, Son Jesus who came to show us the way to salvation threw His being crucified and His resurrection, that whoever believeth in Him shall have eternal life. The New Testament chronicles parts of Jesus' life here on earth, His teaching and the Miracles He performed. It refers to the Gospel as the *Good News Bible*, with written versions of the New Covenant being offered to all humanity for redemption. Also was the belief that the Virgin Mary gave birth to Jesus.

The twelve apostles continued Jesus' teachings. Some wrote accounts and some went on to build churches and cathedrals. Apostle Peter was the first Roman Bishop, as time moved on different sects started to develop from reformed movements. A reformed movement is a different concept of perception on the Scriptures and if one enrolls others into that concept with enough followers it becomes a sect within itself. Martin Luther, 1483-1546 proclaimed through his study and perception of the Scriptures that churches and priests were not the only way to salvation, but that it was our individual Spiritual faith with God. I believe this to be so, that no matter how many doctrines and sects come about, if they are all based on one God for all humanity without any sense of separation, who cares if the sky looks more blue or white it is still the sky that we all look upon. This is not to make less of anyone who finds a doctrine they want to stay with. God gives us free choice because Spirit is all oneness.

Process

List the doctrines you have experienced and your thoughts on them.

Chapter 10

Consciousness to Freedom

Our freedom is in our conscious living in the moment of time we are given. Anything else is an opinion of the past or the future based on a perception of projection. Each moment we embrace, allows our mind to choose consciously and help diminish the destruction of the moment by going unconscious in the past or the future as a habitual reactive reaction. Instead, we are asked to be an observer of our own Spiritual mind and learn to master the Spiritual control God desires for us.

For example: One summer morning I woke up to find a very overcast gloomy day awaiting me. The day before was beautiful and sunny. I however, was so busy cleaning house, washing my dogs, taking coaching calls and tutoring my grandson after school that I hardly had time to really take in the beauty of the day, as it flew by with busyness.

On that gloomy morning, I had expected that since it was summer I would awake to another sunny day, and with most of my chores and counseling calls completed for the week this would be my day to enjoy the garden overlooking the large waterfall into my swimming pool, relaxing and bathing in the sun with the poetry of my choice. Not so, it was not only gloomy and overcast, but cold as well. My first thought was to become a victim of the weather. My ego mind told me I had ripped myself off of the sunshine of the day before and now I had a gloomy depressing cold day ahead of me.

As I poured my potion of victim coffee, I began to think with my Spiritual mind, which is contained in the same container of the ego mind, like a battery with negative and positive, it's still the same battery.

I began to realize it was still a day for Spirit to awaken, and when life gives you what looks like lemons you can always make lemonade. By changing my thought system from ego over to Spirit I began to see the beauty of the day. Instead of labeling it gloomy I called it cozy, instead of feeling sorry that I couldn't enjoy the sun I turned on my electric fireplace, and instead of someone else's poetry I created my own.

There are times that our Spirit wants us to relax and be creative, to go within is to find the silent peace within us, to stop and listen to our own breath of life. Sometimes this happens when we are ill and forced to have bed rest. It is as if Spirit is saying can I please have a moment of your time.

There are lots of illnesses that are connected to the mind and wrong minded thinking of the ego. It has been said that cancer is connected to anger. Back pain has been associated with a thought that turns into a decision of not being supported. Legs, knees or feet pain can indicate a thought of not moving forward in life. A stiff neck can be not looking where you are going. Bad sight can indicate not seeing clearly. These are just a few examples of the ego thought system within the mind. That's why it is important to go to Holy Spirit to guide the mind. For more information on how thoughts affect our bodies, I would recommend Louise Hay's book: "You can heal your life."

I believe true freedom from worry and sadness comes from our inner consciousness of ourselves; to know and accept that within the sub-conscious mind there are thoughts and behaviors that we should not label but to at least acknowledge that they are part of the Human condition of the Spiritual journey.

Process

1. What thoughts do you need to be conscious of for your mental health?

2. What thoughts do you need to be conscious of for your physical health?

Name Your Path to Rome

My name for Spiritual path is called Teacher of Spirit. We are all teachers of Spirit. As we teach we learn, as we learn we teach. I just chose to be more pronounced with my Spiritual teachings and have made a decision to make it my life's career. When we name something in a positive way with Spiritual thinking we breathe life into the idea of how we perceive ourselves. Such as: "I'm a good artist, actor, musician, etc." By training our mind to think of ourselves as well as others in a positive Spiritual way we then become what we think.

I once heard an African minister say that a Spiritual African will wake up in the morning look up at the sky and name the day. That, by naming the day he then lives into that day with the name he has given it, and that each day is looked at as a gift from Spirit to live into from moment to moment until nightfall when one sleeps and then awakens to a new dawn.

A moment is not like a bank account, where you can save it up for the next day. A moment spent, no matter how you spend it is gone forever and the next day the account of the moments is full again. That is why it is senseless to harbor resentment and anger from one day to the next. Ephesian 4-26 "In your anger do not sin; do not let the sun go down while you are still angry."

Process

1. What Ego anger are you holding onto?

2. Turn it over to Spirit mind and write what comes to you.

Roads to Communication

My husband, Clement and I use what is called, communication to deliver. Whenever one of us are angry or upset with each other, or anyone else for that matter, we ask the question do I have communication to deliver, what do I need to say to release myself from it, what am I willing to take responsibility for co-creating my anger and upset, and what do I observe I don't need to take responsibility for? This really helps the *split mind* to step back as an observer of one's mind thinking and in what direction it is going. There are only two directions for it to go, Spiritual or ego, both really being of the same mind.

So, not sleeping on anger or upset helps us to wake up to our right mind thinking, bringing us back to the present moment that is designed to be enlightening, if we move our ego mind aside and allow Spirit to lead. My husband always says: "When I'm hanging onto anger or upset what would Spirit have me do?" In that moment I know I need to let go and let God. Plato wrote in the Republic that the ones that achieve are the ones that have a goal in mind, and are immune to anything other than that goal.

My thoughts are there are many goals for us to have but none as important as forgiveness, which brings Spiritual peace to the universe. So why not have a goal of direct, clear responsible communication with ourselves and others, in order to clear the space for what we really all want, acceptance of who we are, feeling good enough, forgiven and loved. When we forgive, we give up the illusionary right to punish another and we also free ourselves from the heavy burden of anger that will only lead us to the destruction of our peace.

Process

1. Who or what are you upset with?

2. Why do you have this upset?

3. List the communication you want to deliver about the upset.

4. Take action on the communication you want to handle and record the results.

The Road to Truth

What is truth in an illusionary world? Plato wrote in The Republic about the greatest lie. He writes: "What if everything we have been taught and raised with was merely a dream, and during that time we spent deep within the Earth?" I perceive this to mean that we are dreaming our lives on a material earth and that we so believe in our ego's illusionary lies that we have fallen asleep and are in a dream, and have created a consensus reality for it, generation after generation bringing ourselves deeper and deeper into the earth, forgetting the Spiritual world that is here but unseen to most by the naked eye.

The Spirit world is not only within us, it is also around us. The Bible speaks of Spirit in terms of angels, the parting of the Red Sea, the burning bush, manna from heaven, etc. All Spirit comes from One Source, God, but there are many different dimensions of God, all coming from Oneness. God has intermediaries between the material and celestial worlds. In the time of Moses when God spoke to the Hebrews His voice was so overbearing that they covered their ears and begged Moses to ask God to stop speaking. With that in mind could you imagine how intense it would be to look into the face of the One Divine Holy Spirit?

God knows what we can handle, so what we actually see is God; through angels as some of us call them, a Greek word meaning messenger. We tend to romanticize Spiritual messengers as wearing wings and halos with trumpets or harps. Some people believe Spirit guides are different from guardian angels; some refer to them as one in the same. Again dualism shows up, instead of one thought one mind. Whether we call them Spiritual helpers, guardian angels, or Spirit guides, they are still messengers of God, bringing us messages to help us heal and grow toward our consciousness of our true identity.

Example: Maybe you go to apply for a job as a Flight Attendant and you are passed over for the job, feeling sad and rejected you look for employment elsewhere. You find out that there are Spiritual classes being given in order to become an Ordained Minister, something that has always been in the back of your mind. Once you have completed your courses you realize that it is your life's work, and what you love to do, even much more than traveling. This is what happened to me. I remember the day I received the rejection notice. I was so sad and embarrassed. It took weeks to get over it and I kept wondering what I did wrong during the interview. I did nothing wrong, it simply was not on my blueprint chart to become a Flight Attendant. I would eventually travel to wonderful mystical places, but it would be at leisure with my husband in years to come. Had I received the job I may have never met my husband, or made the decision to attend Spiritual College and have the opportunity to teach and write on Spiritual healing.

Call it guardian angel or Spirit guide; Spirit was there to guide me with what I didn't even realize was possible for me, or that on some level that I had made a promise to come to this Earth to help point the Spiritual way as my profession and my passion.

Process

1. When did you experience rejection?

2. What opportunities did it open up for you?

Transition

I always heard if you want to make God laugh; tell him your plans for yourself and exactly how it looks for you. Yes, goal setting is important along with action plans. We need to be open and listen for answers when Spirit calls, by practicing at looking and listening to signs that are given to us, instead of always focusing on material existence that takes us to what we call the end of our lives, with stuff we cannot take with us. Death does not come with a U Haul truck, it comes to pick up our Spirit and move on to what's next, with nothing needed for the journey but perhaps some good Karma from our Life's journey to insure the level of consciousness we would like to move into.

It is all the same energy, but with different levels for future Spiritual growth. I believe that is why we are here, to be spiritually trained for something far greater than we believe ourselves to be, and that oneness is the inner action between the veils of physical and astral existence. One has no impact on the other, for they are one in the same of the Spirit's journey.

People have many different beliefs about death and where it takes you. I believe that as our thoughts create illusionary reality in the life of our body, it also creates the illusionary reality in the death of our body. We move on with our perception to different realms and what we create these perceived realms to be is where we just may create ourselves to be. So, if you believe in Hell and damnation be aware that's where your illusionary perception may take you. If you believe in heaven that's where your illusionary mind will take you. If you believe you will reincarnate back to the world then Hello, you're back. Dust to dust, ashes to ashes may well be your ultimate incubator where you lay your Spirit down.

You are at choice as a Divine Spirit of God, what energy field and plane you will perceive to project yourself into. Every moment of universal energy is thought in process, a thought in one Spiritual mind with billions of fragments belonging to that one source of thought. That is one reason why collective consciousness can help lead the way to one's Spiritual reality, for what would truly be the journey back to Rome. We spend a lot of time going in different directions of what God wants for us here on earth and debating who's right and who's wrong. We even debate where God wants us to journey to after the physical body is gone.

Process

1. What are your perceived thoughts on death?

2. What are your perceived thoughts on an after life?

More Thoughts on Transition

There is no right or wrong on matters that are based on speculation and opinions. We will only know the facts when we arrive spiritually, without the dense body we believe ourselves to be. A Course in Miracles states: "I am not a body; I am as God created me."

In the Bible, John 11:4, there is the account of a man named Lazarus who was sick. When Jesus heard this he said: "This sickness will not end in death no, it is for God's glory so that God's Son may be glorified through it." Jesus is then told that the man Lazarus is dead. Jesus replies to his disciples: "Our friend Lazarus has fallen asleep, but I'm going to wake him up." Jesus also said in the Gospel of John: "I am the resurrection and life. He who believes in Me will live even though he dies, and whoever lives and believes in Me will never die." Jesus then goes to the tomb of Lazarus, has the stone removed and then calls out in a loud voice: "Lazarus come out." Lazarus then came out with his hands and feet wrapped in strips of linen and a cloth around his face. Jesus then said: "Take off the grave clothes and let him go home."

During this time there were many people mourning Lazarus' death for four days, believing him dead and gone forever. Jesus not only shows that dead is a belief of the mind but that after physical death we are still eternal. The name Jesus always reminds me of just us, meaning all of us.

As I write this book I'm experiencing my father passing through the veil of illusionary time of poor health and old age. Each time I visit him I sense two worlds he is living in, one here on earth, and the other slowly moving through the veil to the next level. There is both sadness and beauty in this transformation. Sadness for all of us who love him and will miss him, and beauty in the new Spiritual level he will get to play in with no dense body weighing him down to the belief of illusionary illness, old age and death. He will still be here as one with his loved ones but just on a different ethereal level of existence.

Our thoughts are very important in the evolution of all humanity, and how we come to think about the hereafter and the always is, makes a huge difference in the collective consciousness of what ethereal life will be like. Every day that we experience is a new day for collective consciousness to wake up and to be aware of the Spiritual mind and choose a new Spiritual awakening to all our collective experiences.

By making the choice of forgiveness and love we can make the alterations necessary to heal not only our own illusionary split mind but also the sleeping illusion of the walking dream we have made real to our illusionary thoughts of separation from each other. So, if we begin to see the death of the body as a move to the next level of Spiritual existence, collectively we would experience it on the same level.

My husband, Clement never really believed that contact could be made with someone who has transcended, until his mother, who spent the last six months of life on earth bedridden and passed on at age 97, came to him in a very vivid dream, walking with what he called a strut, looking happy and well. He knew then that it was her message to him that she was moving on to the next level, and that the consciousness that was thought to be lost is actually returning itself to infinite, eternal time and space, forever evolving.

It is us who put time in a capsule, seeing birth and death as a beginning and an end. How frightening can that be to the human psyche, who believes itself to be a dense body? No wonder there is so much sadness, anger and worry to think of just disappearing one day and that's it, the show is over, and goodbye loved ones! If God is the Alpha and the Omega, wouldn't we also be the Alpha and the Omega, since we are part of the Oneness of God? It is all so simple, but our split thoughts of separation keep us imprisoned within our own mind.

Process

1. Does the thought of death scare you? Why or why not?

2. Does the thought of Spiritual eternal life give you peace? Why or why not?

Eternal Oneness

What would be the consequences of believing there is an Eternal Oneness that we all share? That time and space is nothing more than an illusion of the mind? That when we transcend we move to another level of existence, but we are still connected to oneness and that our roles on earth are nothing more than a training camp for something far greater than the ego can ever give us, and that we are only here to learn to tame the ego and move on to self forgiveness of separation? Then, onto our Spiritual quantum self moving forward, backward and forever in time and space because our inheritance is eternal life as Jesus told us it would be, if we only believe? I believe He meant to not only believe in Spirit but to also believe ourselves as Spirit.

Just like when he called out Lazarus name to remind him to wake up, take the grave clothes off and go home. Did Lazarus perceive himself to be dead until he was told he was merely sleeping? Can the power of thought be that powerful? If it is, then wouldn't the same Spiritual thought system that all roads lead to Rome have us give up the struggle of separation, so that we would join thoughts in the present moment instead of devaluing it by looking at a past that has recycled itself to the present moment or the future that is yet to come presenting itself as the present moment? So you see, no matter how we perceive time it's always present in the moment. No matter how many different reincarnations, dimensions or levels of existence there are, we only experience the moment that is.

Process

How could this thought system of illusionary time change your perception of life?

I believe the eyes behold whatever beauty we see in the world and that the thought takes place in the moment of observation.

The eye is the lamp of the body. If your eyes are healthy, your body will be full of light.

Matthew 6:22

Chapter 11

The Road to Resurrection

Can it be that we live in an illusionary world in which we have crucified ourselves within our own split mind, and that the display of Jesus' crucifixion was freedom from the body that contains the split mind, and that His resurrection was a Holy display of Spirit's eternal existence? Resurrection and crucifixion being one and the same of the message He brought to us of ultimate forgiveness for the distortion we believe others bring upon us. Jesus is appealing to the only language we seem to understand, a language of dualism, good and evil, life and death. What Jesus goes on to show is that His body is missing from the tomb but His Spirit is free.

We tend to believe in our illusionary thoughts of death as a final end, that even when Jesus appeared before the disciples and said: "Peace be with you," they were startled and frightened, thinking they saw a ghost. He then said to them: "Why are you troubled, and why do doubts raise in your mind?" Once again Jesus gives an insightful look at the illusionary thought of death and what is possible beyond the veil of what we think to be our reality.

Process

1. Write out the perceived Ego reality you have of yourself.

2. Write out the perceived Spirit reality you have of yourself.

Trans-state

Those of you that have ever watched a hypnosis stage show have actually seen the power of collective consciousness. Starting with a secret bargain of the audience wanting to see people act out in a fashion that is not their own, such as acting like chickens etc. Then there's the power of suggestion to the subconscious mind of the volunteers; people who subconsciously want to act out an uninhibited behavior, different then the controlled conscious behavior known to society as proper behavior. Then, there's the hypnotist who is trained to select a number of people from a count of twenty volunteers, selecting the most subjective ones to work with. No one is doing anything they do not want to do or be. It is not a trance that is beyond their control.

In hypnosis we are still at choice, but for entertainment of an audience of collective consciousness this becomes an illusion much the way we live life under a hypnotic state of habit and illusion, and that is the way many of us experience birth and death. A baby is born, a person dies. Every day we put ourselves through self hypnosis by what we think and what we say, and unfortunately a lot of it is ninety per cent negative and ten per cent positive. Advertisements capitalize on the negative Subconscious mind; if you don't use this dish washing detergent you will be embarrassed by the spots on your drinking glasses in front of your guests, or if your mouth wash is not this brand you will have bad breath.

I'm not attacking advertisements; they just work with what they know they have; a collective consciousness of minds that believe themselves to be a dense body. Notice there are no commercials pleading for collective Spiritual consciousness for a product. We do at this time have telecasting evangelists and special programs and talk shows working at getting our collective consciousness together.

The only problem is the thought system of separation that one's road is the only road that will lead us to Rome, so what we get is mass confusion as to who is right and who is wrong, then the debate and hypnotic illusion of separation takes place. Hypnosis starts in our own mind; there is no force outside of us convincing us of our thoughts. It is a choice of what we believe.

When Jesus walked on water He was in a super-conscious trans-state of thinking, where anything is possible. We have heard of fire walks or breaking bricks in half by hand; these are trans-states of super-consciousness. Learning any new task involves the conscious

108

mind to perceive itself to a higher level of skill and knowledge, which is inheritably ours to grasp hold of. Jesus was always in the grasp of His super-conscious state. He knew His true natural state of wholeness when He performed what we call miracles.

When the disciple Peter saw Jesus walking on water, Peter requested to come over to Him, and Jesus replied: "Come." Peter then got down out of the boat, walked on water over to Jesus but when he saw the wind he was afraid and beginning to sink, he cried out: "Lord save me," immediately Jesus reached out His hand and caught him. "You of little faith," Jesus said, "Why do you doubt?"

In our super-conscious state there is nothing to doubt but doubt itself which comes from fear of the unknown. Fear then sends super-conscious thoughts to illusionary lower levels of thoughts. So, Peter within his mind, went from what was possible, to fear of what he thought was impossible, and that was with one of the greatest teachers showing him what could be achieved. This is what a lot of us Spiritual beings on this human journey do; we make major super-conscious strides, only to pull ourselves back like a rubber band with illusionary consciousness of fear. When this happens we temporarily lose grasp of our true Spiritual powers, as one with God, we begin to hypnotize our mind to think in the "I can't" trance as opposed to the "I can" trance; when in reality there is nothing the great Creator has not given us to access the power within us.

Process

1. What "I can't" trans-state do you habitually practice?

2. What "I can" trans-state would you be willing to practice daily?

3. Record your progress as you practice them daily.

It is never too late to change the compass of the road you are on

How great it is to know that at any time we can reinvent ourselves, simply by changing our mind and following our right mind thinking which leads us to identify our own hypnotic trance we have put ourselves under. Every day we do this in one form or another. Sometimes it's the same routine of waking up, having a cup of coffee, driving to work, coming home, watching TV, or getting on our computers etc.

We also use this trans-state within our mind; what we think about, the people we encounter, and most importantly what's going on in our thought system that then becomes our feelings and emotions extracting out a persona of who we believe ourselves to be. Unfortunately, some of it is not very empowering and for a great number of people at the core is the inner conversation of "not good enough." Not the right career, house, car, age, looks, relationship, weight, success, and so on and so on goes the list of trans-states we put ourselves under, when all along we have the power within us, given to us by the Holy Spirit to transfer the illusionary trans-state to the Spiritual mind, where all is possible.

Have you ever called a phone number often and no matter how many times you call this number you still look it up in your phone book? Then, one day you're so tired of having to look up the number that you take the five minutes to read it aloud combine the numbers and memorize it, and from that point on your trans-state kicks in and instead of going to your phone book you go to your mind. You have now developed a new hypnotic way to manifest that number. We can call this the dehypnotizing in order to re-hypnotize and use it in all areas of our lives, like unwanted habits and thoughts.

When I was a little girl I belonged to a family of ten. We were raised to be good law abiding people in society with a good sense of humor, but that was about it. Everything else from that point I needed to make up for myself. Of course that was after I got off the victim band wagon of the past and started to create myself as I always wanted to be and I learned that I could use new trans-habits toward the goals I wanted to create.

Correction of the Ego/Spirit Mind

One was music, as a little girl there was always a piano in the house. No one used it or was taught to use it. I remember sitting at it and wishing I could play just one little piece of music. As I got older I thought my ship had sailed and I would never learn to play the piano, that only lucky little girls received piano lessons. Then one day as an adult I was in a consignment store and there before my eyes was a baby grand piano. Right there and then I shifted my trans-state of poor little girl who went without piano lessons and only looked at a piano day after day and wished she could play at least one little tune, to the adult woman buying her own baby grand and enrolling herself in lessons to learn more than just one little tune. Liberace I'm not, but the moments of oneness and happiness with my little tunes give me a sense of achievement and joy.

It is the same with education, as a teen it was hard to keep me interested in studies. Now as an adult I can't get enough education, on how the mind works and the Spiritual aspects of our being. So, we can always revisit the child within us and parent that child to create all that we want and know we can be. Self hypnosis is our personal key to our own mental attitudes and how we carry them out; the suggestibility will be there in the ego mind, our job is to shift it to Spirit mind which is the One True Mind of God.

Try this for twenty eight continuous days with any habit of negative thought pattern and see your trans-state change, leading you to Spiritual concentration and focus.

Process

1. Ask your inner child what it feels it missed out on.

2. Ask your inner child what you can do to receive that for them.

3. Write down action steps it would take to do this.

4. Record your results.

Counselor Within

Jesus said: "I leave with you a Counselor." The Counselor Jesus was referring to was the Counselor within. The Counselor within is always with us, wherever we go, there we are. Getting used to this concept was at first upsetting for me. No matter how many designer handbags or shoes I possessed, or whatever extravagant experience I encountered, there I was; the same insides viewing a different outside and internalizing it through the thoughts of my insides; sounds pretty messy doesn't it? Well that's where the Counselor within comes into play, to help us choose the right thought system of any and all conditions we find ourselves in.

Our consciousness comes from our thoughts and our personality comes from the thought of who we think ourselves to be, using the world as a mirror to look upon that reflection. Each individual who does this contributes to the collective consciousness of confusion and the manifestation of an unreal world into existence that then gets internalized into emotions leading to actions of confused separation. When in actuality separation does not really exist, because we have only one Counselor within all of us. Some may call the Counselor by different names, the Holy Spirit, Intuition, the Higher Self, Divine Guidance, etc, but it is only One Counselor providing different roads to choose from. We all have within us the ability to answer the call if we silence the mind long enough to hear the sound of our own internal trumpet.

I have always found that a general knowledge of different roads to Rome can be extremely beneficial for better understanding and appreciation for all modalities and classifications of the journey to Spiritual wisdom that leads us back to who we really are! One with God!

Everything outside of that is all made up and becomes a trans-state in which we live into, always looking for evidence to make the unreal real in our mind. When we stop trying to make other Spiritual practices wrong and realize the oneness in all, we will make a monumental difference for humanity. Again, this takes a general knowledge of understanding and non-judgmental attitudes toward our fellow brothers and sisters, and looking for the basic foundation, Love and Forgiveness through the Holy Spirit within all of us.

While studying hypnosis in order to be a certified hypnotist, I became very interested in the works of Milton Erickson, MD. I was amazed how he weaved hypnotic suggestions into story telling. The

114

story would not be about the client but centered on something the client could identify with in and around whatever problem they felt they were experiencing. It would bring them into a trans like state where their sub-conscious mind could be tapped into with positive suggestibility and the results were amazing.

If we think about it, we are in a world of suggestibility, day in and day out. Even the Biblical Scriptures are told in a suggestible way, and the suggestion is always what the mind can conceive, it can achieve. Take for instance, the story of Jonah and the whale. We can perceive that Jonah was in the belly of a whale or we can perceive that the story is a metaphor for feeling as if he was swallowed up with rebellion and indecision and feeling like he was in the belly of a whale. The Bible doesn't spell it out to us, it allows us our own personalization of perception based on our sub-conscious thinking in order to lead us to higher consciousness of what's Spiritually possible for us to achieve.

So many Spiritual modalities and people have different perceptions to the same suggestion of the refinement of creation and that our higher self teaches and trains us through the lessons of our earthly life and is preparing us for a much greater picture than we ever perceived ourselves to be as part of the whole universal concept of One.

We transcend through the wheel of life toward self realization of what our part on earth is and what we decided before physical birth, and what we will leave as a Spiritual legacy to others before transcending to the next level of universal consciousness.

I believe we are like a drop of rain in the ocean adding and creating a ripple of energy to the whole body of water, and that every single one of us is important to the whole of creation and the illusion of separation. We may ask, how did this happen and when did this happen; for that we can again go back to Genesis the Biblical story of creation, the rise and fall of the illusionary fall within the mind can be found between the lines. Our reading between lines and thinking outside the lines is what will help us understand our purpose for healing and finding wholeness, not only in ourselves but also in the wheel of life, transforming ourselves back to perfection where we have the choice to aid others back to our Spiritual home.

Process

1. Read Genesis as a way of decoding the illusionary fall of man.

2. Write out a short synopsis of your thoughts on it. Do not judge yourself wrong or right; just explore your own inner thoughts.

Our treasures are within us. That is something that can never be taken away as long as we believe ourselves as pure Spirit. That is where the buried treasures are.

Do not store up for yourselves treasures on earth where moth and rust destroy and where thieves break in and steal.

Matthew 6:19

Chapter 12

Does Life Really Exist On Other Planes

Jesus spoke these words to the apostles when He knew His life on earth was near the end: "Do not let your hearts be troubled, trust in God, trust also in Me. In My Father's house are many rooms. If it were not so I would have told you. I'm going there to prepare a place for you and if I go and prepare a place for you I will come back and take you to be with Me that you also may be where I am. You know the way to the place where I am going." John 14 1-4. He was assuring us that we need not trouble our mind with thoughts of separation, for it would be only an illusion that He would cease to exist, and that it would only be the physical eye that would not see Him on earth. In Spirit though, He would always remain with us in order to help show us the way home, which we already know but have mistakenly forgotten.

He also said: "There are many rooms in My Father's house." Is he referring to different planes of existence? My understanding is that He is speaking about different planes of existence, and preparation is part of it through the life lessons that we learn. He also said: "You know the way to the place where I am going." That is part of our knowingness. What we know that we know, that there is a greater Source than ourselves. A Source we are all a part of, a universal consciousness of all that is.

Unfortunately our mind of illusion believes in an unreal world of death and separation. What Jesus is saying is there is no separation between life and death, just different rooms within the house; the house still being the house, and the rooms being part of the whole of the house. Jesus said: "I will come back and take you to be with Me, that you also may be where I am." My perception about this statement is that, when we wake up to our Oneness we will no longer perceive loss or separation in the wholeness, thereby creating a belief in an ongoing energy source that would move in one direction with different dimensions moving along with it and that it is only the illusionary mind viewing it as a different dimension.

Take our nightly sleep, for instance. Do we actually go unconscious, for up to eight hours or do we astral travel though dimensions and back again, and why at sleep time? Because, that is when we are allowing our subconscious mind to rest with all its data and precepts about the illusionary world and thereby entering into the real world where anything and everything is possible. What we believe is what we design ourselves to be; so if we believe that there is only one life for us on earth we will live a life out of that concept, but if we believe in an afterlife that is what we will live into.

So the question of: Does life exist on other plains is a matter of what we allow our mind to perceive. I personally love the concept, that there are Spirit guides and angels guiding us, and that everything that is designed and invented here on earth has first taken place on a Spiritual level and brought here by Spirit guides who help us to be at the right place at the right time assisting us to take action on our dreams, goals and commitments for giving back to the planet and humanity. Sometimes the guides bring in a child prodigy to make sure the assignment is complete, so humanity has what it needs at a particular time and space. So, around and around it goes striving for home and paradise once more.

What about harmful inventions, like nuclear bombs, etc? Well, that's when the world of illusion starts with fear of survival because of thoughts of separation instead of one world, one God that we are all a part of. Even if we encounter aliens from other planets, would they not be part of the whole universe, which is the God Energy? It is only illusion that has us think separated thoughts that dis-empower us and the world. When collective consciousness experiences its true state of one Great Spiritual Energy of God, then and only then can we rub away the ego which will free us of bondage so we can experience ourselves as we were originally made by God and part of God, leading to the parts of the whole pie.

When we look to keep it simple, it's one Spiritual thought at a time, learning to choose and recognize the thoughts that cause dis-ease from the ego mind or a thought that brings love and peace of mind, with no fear of separation which is of the Spirit mind and working from that mind is the true road to Rome.

Process

1. Write your thoughts on other planes of existence.

2. What has you believe in these concepts?

Chapter 13

Relationship

Let's look at the word relationship and its meaning. Relating or being related connected, being of the same family or kin. We are all related when we realize we come from the same Creator, but just like there were different tribes described in Scriptures there are different cultures and families, all belonging to the whole of humanity. Coupling has always been a part of our being, from the creation of Adam and Eve onward. This is how the Human species continues to reproduce itself, two halves creating a whole, but even after the instinct to reproduce most human beings still desire a mate and sometimes feel an incompletion in their lives without one. Of course there are exceptions to every rule, but the consensus is they desire a mate.

Most of what we are looking for is lost parts of our own self love that through the mirror of another's eyes we can see a reflection of love. In actuality how much we love and accept our self is to the degree of what we will attract to us. Love replaces fear and if we fear not being lovable or good enough we look for love to replace fear, but the one mistake we can make is looking for it in special relationships, which add to the separation of who we decide to love leaving us open to fear if the special relationship does not work or provide us with the love we thought would handle the fear.

Within all of us is Gods eternal love, it lives in us, it is never missing. The thought that turns emotions into experience of not being lovable or good enough is of the ego mind who wants us to limit our love to specialness and underneath that is: "How can I get more love for myself through special love." This is an illusionary thought system that keeps love for all mankind at a distance by putting it in containers, separating it and limiting love for all humanity, rationalizing why we fear or hate certain beings on earth and if we are feeling fear or hate it only cancels out the feeling of love providing the space to encourage separation.

We tend to use the world as a mirror for what we are feeling inward. If the world sees us as attractive we feel attractive. If the world sees us as overweight by definition of fashion magazines we feel overweight. We often look outside of us to feel what we are feeling inside of us, therefore being a robot to humanity. We must remember perceptions are not facts and often lead to misconceived notions of what is real. Thoughts are formless until we put the meaning into them. It is the observation that creates the thought into an image, which then becomes the experience. True knowledge comes when we recognize past thoughts that are meaningless to the journey forward and choose to change them in the present moment as an extension toward our Spiritual growth.

Process

1. What meanings are you putting to the thoughts about yourself?

2. Are these empowering thoughts? If not what new thoughts are you willing to create?

Self Love

I have always said if I had known what I know now about relationship, I wouldn't have had to say goodbye so many times in order to find something greater. The greater was always within me. No one can complete us; we can only complete our self by knowing that we are loved as God created us. Everything else is a perception of love, and if we make it to be who we are by saying I'm in love, we begin to make the separation within ourselves.

Just about everyone finds the beginning of a relationship intoxicating, like fairy dust, but as time continues it settles into a familiar, comfortable love, the love we have always known as just being there. Judgments we make about ourselves for not being in love or not having a special relationship is nothing more than a perception of what our ego mind has conceived of love.

The ego mind lives because we allow it. If each one of us, one smile at a time, corrected a thought from ego over to Spirit we would overcome the ego mind and raise the consciousness of what love is, and the world would become a forgiving playground of wholeness for all of humanity. If we are what we think, why not choose the Spirit mind that will lead the way home to inner peace. Isn't that what we truly want, and not the false reflection of happiness though the world of illusion? Therefore anyone or anything cannot falsely leave us without love, which is impossible because our true identity is one with God's forgiveness and Love.

Process

1. List the ways you are willing to love yourself.

2. List the ways you are willing to love others.

3. Write down what the consequences will be.

Chapter 14

Questions and Answers

What replaces our illusions in an unreal world that feels real?

What will replace them will be our observations, which then will have us create our thoughts, which then turn to emotions, images and experiences that occur real. If you don't like what you're feeling or the experience change the thought.

How do I change my thought?

You change your thought by knowing that you have an illusionary split mind; one that is of ego thought and one that is of Spirit thought and consciously observing and choosing Spirit. Again, the only reason ego exists is because we allow it to. Both are of one mind because there is no duality, we perceive duality and that's how it seems to exist.

Process

1. List your dual thoughts that keep you in a quandary (two opposing thoughts occurring at the same time, such as one of the Spirit one of the ego).

2. Transform them into a singular thought (Use Spirit thought).

3. Write down the clarity you receive.

Correction of the Ego/Spirit Mind

How do I keep my thoughts in Spirit mind?

You keep your thoughts in Spirit mind the same way you get to Carnegie Hall; Practice, practice practice. Within twenty eight to twenty nine days of a moon cycle, you should be pretty much aware of your thoughts, whether they are accompanied by Spirit or ego. From there you create, produce and act within your Spiritual script you design yourself to be.

Process

1. Keep a 28 day journal of any situation where you intentionally chose Spirit mind thinking over ego mind thinking. Record them nightly.

<u>28 day journal process</u>

Correction of the Ego/Spirit Mind

How will I know my Spirit thought from my ego thought?

You will know your Spirit thought from your ego thought by the way you feel. Your thought becomes your emotion. If you feel fearful, upset, anguish, anger etc., you will know you have chosen the Ego mind. On the other hand, if you feel in that same situation faith, peace, forgiveness and love you will have chosen the Spirit mind.

What if the ego tries to hold onto me?

If you feel like the ego is trying to hold on to you then you are being a victim. Remember, we always have free choice to choose ego versus Spirit.

Who will I be without ego thoughts?

You will be a Spiritual being on a human journey to learn lessons for further Spiritual growth, not only for yourself but for all humanity. God wants us to find our way back home because He knows we never really left home at all. Learning how to apply these principles is very important toward our Spiritual growth. If we ask the questions in this chapter to ourselves and answer them with our Spiritual consciousness, we will raise the vibration of our Spiritual mind. Until now, we have thought ego to be an automatic thrown to. Spirit will turn negative into positive one moment at a time; this will take practice and patience as does anything worth achieving, until it becomes a staple of who you really are.

Ernest Holmes wrote that Shakespeare is accredited with the saying: "There is nothing either good or bad, but thinking it makes it so." It is one thing to know a principle, another to apply it. I believe that our human journey into self realization is to first rid the mind of its divided nature so it can embrace the limitless opportunities available and know that there are no lost opportunities, for to think this way is to think with a divided mind.

What is a thought?

A thought is a mental activity within the mind that observes, thinks and creates ideas, notions and imaginings through consideration of reflections from a mirror world outside itself, bringing back mental activities or opinions in which to perceive a thought. It can also be reflections or recollections from the past. A thought can be an intention of the future conceived in the mind. A conscious thought is a thought taken at the moment of observation. We call this a mindful thought.

Many of us seem to live in past reflections through the illusionary world, coming up with observations and imaginings about ourselves, not really knowing who our true self is because we are so busy worrying how we appear to the outside world and not realizing that it is the inside that creates the outside, all being one. So, when choosing our thoughts it is wiser to observe and choose the mindful, at the moment thought that bypasses the formless past and creates intention of a future desired; if we desire to see ourselves in a new light then that will come from within our knowledge, and unlimited truth. We are either attracting self love or repelling it by our thoughts. Remember, time is formless. It is only that which we use to measure our experience here on earth. Thoughts are formless as well; they too are used as a measure of experience.

So now that we know thoughts are a measure of experience, how can we harness them?

We can harness them at the moment of observation. First realizing you are observing it, becoming conscious to where it's coming from, past emotions or future fear. Then, bring yourself back to the present and choose from a clean slate mind, where you have the knowledge and ability that we all have to choose wisely, gauging it by what you are feeling. (Sad, angry etc. dis-empowered thoughts). (Happy, peaceful etc. empowered thoughts,) and it's all power.

I understand that there are times where life brings unexpected sadness or pain. In times like this it is still important to stay engaged in the moment that is, by being ok with what is and knowing that this too shall pass. How we hold onto it and learn from it will extend into our future thoughts of harnessing the moment.

What we want to do is implant thoughts that are relative to what we desire to be manifested. To master our thoughts is to manifest ourselves into a desired existence. This thought started with God, we were and are a thought of God, a perfect creation of His Divine Light. In Genesis, God spoke His thoughts in words which then turned His ideas into formation. We have that capability to create through our thoughts, but before we create form from the formless we must be mindful of our ability to know our true selves, by directing the Soul with Spiritual mind.

The phrase: "Save your soul" comes from the belief that giving your thoughts to Spirit which is Universal Oneness of God, we lead it back to its infinite Self in which it never left. It is Spirit that leads and soul that follows because it relies on free choice, Spirit versus ego. soul does not choose on its own. You may have heard the phrase: "Deep down in my soul, I know what I know," that's because when split mind connects with Spirit mind instead of ego mind, it comes full circle to its true self. Soul is the servant, Spirit is the master, and ego mind is the false self that believes in duality and separation. Body is the flesh known also as the temple, it completes the physical being. The body cannot go on without Spirit. The soul follows the Spirit, a soul may reincarnate many times until Spirit leads it home, each time learning by its karmic mistakes and finding a better way by choosing Spirit mind more and more until it evolves into its self realization of its oneness. From that point anything is possible as infinite Spiritual beings.

What happens to me and the personality I think myself to be?

As you change your thoughts from one moment to the next, staying present to that moment you become aware of two masters at hand; ego being the false master who believes in illusions, and Spirit being your true self living in mastery. Your personality is your persona of who you think you are plus an accumulation of all that you have dreamed up to this point, bringing into account your culture, education, beliefs and upbringing. Ego is of a personal nature. We all have one and it is only rubbed away when we consciously do so and embrace our Spiritual nature.

We use our personality for believing in separation. This is not a cosmic occurrence, it a personal occurrence. It is what we look at as a distinction of who we are, based on our thought system and using the outside world to look at our reflection as the final judgment of who we are. We are always looking for evidence of our individuality; Like: "That's just who I am. Like me or leave me. No one ever understands me." When we accumulate all these different thoughts, collectively what we have is mass separation from the whole. When God said: "I Am the I Am" is simply, I am all with Universal Oneness. So, the worry about the personality is of the little ego mind that cannot see outside itself. It knows it will fade like an old film when we stop contemplating upon it. If we continue contemplating on it, it's like adding constant restoration to it. We will not lose our self to the personality that holds us in bondage and sometimes a victim, but what we will find is something far greater and that is truth and knowledge of our true Spirit which will recreate and design the Spiritual us that we are.

Process

1. Make a list of what you perceive your personality to be.

2. How is that showing up in your life?

3. List any changes you would like to make.

4. Take action on those changes and list your results.

What if I don't want to be like everyone else?

No two stars are exactly alike. No two grains of sand are exactly alike. So, in our Spiritual nature we are always part of the whole, but we will not be exacts. There will be different callings and different expressions of love and forgiveness, etc. It will be alright as long as we remain the sum of the total consciousness.

Process

1. How do you see yourself as different from others?

2. How are you willing to see commonality in yourself and others?

Correction of the Ego/Spirit Mind

What if I feel alone in my Spiritual quest?

Now we know what Jesus had to contend with when He came to show us the way. Fortunately, He left with us the Counselor within. So He has already paved the way for us. That was over two thousand years ago. Look how much we have advanced, what we have available to us, with freedom of speech and the old world dogma falling away, and all the Spiritual teachings that are available to us now. No more secret hidings or witch burnings, we have Spiritual freedom to connect with the universal oneness, through whatever loving forgiving road leads us back home, where God is waiting with His knowledge that we never really left. He will be there when we wake up from the dream of separation, with angels cheering us onward!

Now that I'm on this road, what happens now?

Now that you are on this road you are now as God created you to be, a Spiritual being with no false illusions of a reality you made up in your thoughts. You are now ready to be a living testament of Christ consciousness, just by being your Spiritual self and by doing so you raise the vibrations of the energy flow that comes into your thoughts like radio waves. Others notice the love and peace you have to offer and want to tune into your station just by you being you, who now knows what thought system to choose.

The atmosphere contains all thoughts and images. Any image you see was first a thought from the mind. These thoughts are tiny little particles that create density. We often say when a person does not realize something that he or she is dense of mind, because that person is using a continuation of thought from a past time to experience the present moment. From that past continuation of thought no new data can be received. It would be like listening to one radio station and trying to get another one in clearly at the same time. We all know that what we would have is just static. So, to get another clear form of energy's vibration we inactivate one to receive another. This opens up the space for new possibilities available to us for new information, what's possible with this new information, and how can it be utilized?

What about my mental habits?

A habit is a tendency to a continual thought, which is also referred to as a thrown to; an unconscious decision set into motion then followed into completion regardless of the outcome of the continual experience. A change of habit would be to sense the unconscious thought, bring it to the surface of Spirit thought system and choose to change the tendency that set the actions and results in motion to your desired completion.

This is done by learning to allow yourself to feel your inner self, not by judgment but by forgiveness that will give you the courage to relocate your true identity within. Identity is a result of experience. When you observe your mental experience you change your thoughts and identity to its true form of love and forgiveness for yourself and others.

Process

1. What mental habits do you want to change?

2. What action steps are you willing to take for manifestation of this change?

3. What will be the outcome?

What about my physical body?

Your physical body is your temple where your soul resides while you're here on earth. If you are here to make a difference in humanities way of thinking for yourself and others, you need a form in which you can be seen. This form will be an image of your inner thoughts about yourself. Our form is maintained in our mind and reflected outward like a mirror. What we really are is Spiritual matter forming a body as a dense vehicle in an illusionary world that works as a classroom to advance our souls. The Science of Mind, by Ernest Holmes believes we have a body within a body to infinity, and I would agree with that.

While we are here to be conscious, we need something to be conscious of, and that includes the body. Perhaps that's why we are so preoccupied with ourselves. We have become our own little play toys while we are here on earth and forgetting the chosen reason we are here, which is to reclaim our inheritance as one with God and to know and live by that one truth, instead of preoccupying ourselves with false Ego thoughts of an illusionary world of pain and suffering.

If we do not change our thoughts about our body, this makes the body a painful experience for our soul. So, it is Spirit who wakes us up to claim our true mission on earth. The Science of Mind also states that living man never dies because inner man is constantly forming matter into a shape of a body. Vedanta also believes that we reincarnate again and again until we reach true enlightenment, I would also agree. The mind is expressed through life and the body is the vehicle of the mind, so whatever you design your physical body to be remember, you are doing it with your thoughts.

Those of you, who may be suffering from an illness, please do not take offense. I only ask you to be open to the possibility of healing your mind of thoughts that could be hindering your health. I'm reminded of the Biblical story of the woman who bled for many years and by touching the robe of Jesus was healed. I ask; was it the robe of Jesus or her faith and the thought that both Jesus and the touch of the robe would heal her? When Jesus turned around and asked who touched His robe, both knew she was healed by her thoughts of faith. This was how many of His miracles were performed through thoughts of Spiritual faith.

So, we can think our body to be healthy along with action steps of nurturing it with the right thoughts, foods and exercising it for firm structure. This would be aligning our thoughts with actions to manifest the outer image we reflect to the world of form, only as a vehicle for dense matter to be the mirror of the body others see.

When we leave this planet all that is gone is the form. The Spirit lives on. Knowing this, we can loosen up on the desperation of the body's mirror to the world and know that death is not the last stop. This knowledge of our true Identity will free us.

The Hebrews wandered forty years in the desert going in circles. This too can be looked at as a metaphor to finding true identity. Why the desert? Because, you could imagine how isolated and hot it may have been, so much so that they almost chose to go back into the bondage of slavery, inspite of all the miracles Spirit provided for them.

Sometimes we do this with our body; we may abuse it with excess food, alcohol, or drugs and lack of exercise, resulting in putting our thoughts on bondage and resentment of the body. We have a choice to change the thought that leads to the image made in the illusionary world. The best advice I can give is to keep positive, loving, forgiving thoughts on your mind, body and soul through Spirit mind thinking and you will not have to obsess about the physical body. You will know form is meaningless and that it is you who put the meaning to it with your observations and thoughts.

Our observations and thoughts multiply into beliefs that are perceived as real. The mind is also meaningless without direction. Given the right direction it is infinite in power and what it can create. Giving it the wrong direction it is self serving and an imprisonment to the soul.

Process

1. What are your thoughts about your body?

2. What positive thoughts are you willing to empower it with?

3. What actions steps are you willing to take to empower it?

4. Record results.

Correction of the Ego/Spirit Mind

How can I contain my Ego mind?

If you look at your mind like a container with a divider down the middle, one side labeled ego the other side labeled Spirit; each time you have an observation leading to thought you get to choose what side of the container to put the thought in. Whichever side fills up the most will be how much weight your thoughts contain, with ego versus Spirit. Now, if with practice we fill the ego side less and less the possibility of having it empty at some point would have Spirit mind in full force, where the ego side would be of no use, it would remain but with nothing to fill it.

Process

1. Write down a time you chose Spirit mind over ego mind, what were the results?

2. How can you choose your Spirit mind over ego mind more consistently?

3. Record the results you are achieving.

Correction of the Ego/Spirit Mind

Isn't the ego necessary?

No it is not. It has no use once we have connected with Spirit mind. It will not need to defend us because there will be nothing to defend. The thought of fear, sin and guilt is manufactured in the ego thought system and what feeds it collectively is when we buy into this and we believe it to be necessary against attack to protect ourselves. As we dim its light into darkness we become what we truly are, a Spiritual light that shines into infinity. It is one mind one thought that is our salvation. We have the power to turn our reluctant energy into receptive energy, by allowing Spirit mind to take the lead. <u>What we believe will take form.</u>

Process

1. Write down a time when something you believed in was manifested through Spirit mind.

2. Write a new dialogue today using the end of negative to start a new positive empowering dialogue. Remember, that only ego needs the body to control an illusionary world, and Spirit only uses body as a means of a vehicle in which to unite with humanity on the level of matter, which we have programmed ourselves to see as reality.

What about other people's thoughts of the illusionary world?

We can only be responsible for our own thoughts of reality. Each time we are responsible, we increase the energy for others to do so. We are not of this world but we are in this world, so we become a Spirit of inner light and surround ourselves with right mind thinking and people who will be attracted to us, or we will teach and encourage right mind thinking by our actions and the way we show up in life.

If you want love and forgiveness then be love and forgiveness. This is what super conscious thinking is. It is thinking beyond the illusionary pain of small mind and meditating on our Infinite mind through our daily moment to moment thoughts, stopping to consciously observe what we are perceiving. Perception is the liquor of life. It can't change the experience but it can change how you deal with the experience and how you relate to other people's perceptions.

Process

1. How do you deal with other's ego perceptions (beliefs)?

2. List the ways you can Spiritually deal with other's ego perceptions (beliefs)?

Leaving the road of life's negative imprints

It isn't always easy to remember a simple rule like: take each present moment for what it is; and what it is becomes what you decide by where you place the thought, ego or Spirit. The imprints we have collected from childbirth on have accumulated in our subconscious mind and feel very familiar to our memory cells, like when we tend to choose people who are like our parents or someone from the past, to recreate an experience of familiarity. Leaving the past where it belongs and waking up to the present moment at hand takes discipline.

As I was writing this book there were and are many other books on living in the present and realizing life as an illusion, with one mind and one Universal God. Each time a new book was on the best seller list I would ask myself, has my book already been written by someone else, and out of that thought, discouragement would arise. But, as I would wake up to the present moment I realized, of course when it comes to Spirituality there is nothing new under the sun.

We are actually going into the archives for information and that a concept continues to grow by continual activity in its belief and sharing it. It doesn't matter how many times it is shared, it's something that needs to be shared in different ways by different people for different listenings, while knowing if we accept the underlying truth that the information is within all of us and we just need to access it from within for practical application.

That which is hidden no longer needs to be hidden. We can now talk and write about true Spirituality and not have to accept dogmatic controlling preaching on what God is. Fortunately churches are becoming more open and accepting to what is called new thought but is actually old thought. If we read the Scriptures with the concept of Universal Oneness we will be able to better enjoy and understand what its implication really is; a sign post that leads us in contemplation of Spiritual growth that helps mankind look for the truth.

Whether you believe it or not or simply use it as a metaphor for inner growth its value is worth its weight in gold, as long as we have the freedom to perceive it not as a book of heaven and hell but as a book of inner growth. Take the duality out of it and look upon it as a book of stirring the human mind to Spiritual thinking and knowledge that heaven is within and paradise will be found when Christ consciousness is reclaimed.

Process

1. Write down your thoughts and beliefs about Spirituality.

2. Where do your thoughts and beliefs generate from?

3. What are the current consequences of these beliefs?

Waking Up From the Dream of Illusion

I believe we are waking up from the dream of illusion, and that the reason we keep receiving the same information written differently but basically being the same is because there is a Universal Energy working with humanity, and it wants teachers to help spread the *good news* on a larger scale in order to get to the masses, as Jesus did with the sermon on the mount and other gatherings.

Now is the best time to live in because there is so much technology available to us. Everything is going faster, no more pony express. We have the internet, faxes, email, cell phones, text messaging and so on. How quickly we can receive messages from just about anywhere in the world. Jesus many times traveled on foot from town to town and was also schooling his disciples who were not always so quick to catch on. He has left with us the Counselor within and we have more technology available than ever before to share our inner knowing, that we are part of the Whole Universal Oneness.

So yes, we are ready for the Second Coming if we continue raising the awareness of consciousness that it will take. We have been given all the supplies to reach the masses, but first we need to reach within ourselves and ask the question: "Have I read enough books, listened to enough tapes, radio shows and seminars to take action on what I know to be my true identity?" I am not saying stop exercising your mind with knowledge. What I am saying is; are you ready to get off the bleachers and get into the game. I pray so, because we are all on the same universal team and paradise is awaiting us from within.

Process

1. How can you contribute to higher consciousness as a teacher of oneness?

2. Write down action steps for your contribution.

3. What is your motivation behind your contribution?

To be meek is to not take offense, because there is nothing real to take offense to. Being in the moment helps to control the conscious mind to it's humble Spiritual essence.

Blessed are the meek, for they shall inherit the Earth.

Matthew 5:5

Chapter 15

The Road to Realization

We are not chaos.

Definition of chaos: Complete disorder.

Chaos is something we all live with in some form or another. We each have our own personal chaos going on within our mind. Even if it is physical, it is still created somewhere within the mind of thoughts, that turn into feelings and then turn into physical and psychological emotions.

We are like aliens on planet earth; our souls are trapped in bodies that long for Spiritual happiness. Some of us have mistaken material gain for happiness, only to find the empty void is still there. Others may have crossed this road and know there is nothing outside of self that will create Spiritual contentment. Sometimes this can be even more painful until it gets better, knowing that you are the creation of your own mind is to take full responsibility for your own actions of forgiveness, not only to others but primarily to yourself, for how can you forgive others if you do not first forgive your own wrong thinking mind.

Knowing to choose wisely between the split mind that is actually one mind is to practice, practice practice, and what we contemplate on we get good at, like a concert pianist who devotes all their time and effort to be the best they can be with the talent, knowledge, notes and chords that are available. This does not only apply to the pianist but to all of us in whatever we do.

I say the most important task we attend to each day is who we are as Spiritual beings and the rest will come when we let go and let God. No, I do not mean to say just sit on a mountain top in a lotus position chanting. What I do mean is; there is a cosmic law of attraction when our mind is set on the goal of Spiritual contentment we allow the universe to serve up opportunities for growth in all areas of our life.

Process

Ask yourself these questions and write down your answers:

1. What is your chaos?

2. Where does your chaos live? (Example) Stomach, heart, head, kidney etc.)

3. What is it you're looking outside yourself to heal?

4. What is it you have to say and do to heal it?

5. Would you know who you were without your chaos?

6. What are you trying to be right about with your chaos?

7. What does your chaos cost you?

8. What would your life be like without chaos?

9. Are you willing to start this new life?

10. What will be your action steps?

11. How and when will you implement them?

12. What will be the wins of doing this?

Tell a friend, someone who champions you and ask them to hold you accountable for what you say you want and what you will do to attain it. Check in with your support team or person weekly, and in six weeks ask yourself what have been your new wins around the chaos now that you have identified and changed your thoughts.

Comprehension

An idea can only go to the level in which it is understood; the greater the comprehension the greater the knowledge. If one remains at one's own level of understanding nothing new is gained in the way of knowledge, but if one rises to the level of new understanding of the new idea new comprehension will lead to new knowledge.

I believe that is what divides the Bible and religions, Old Testament versus New Testament. There seems to be a level of understanding that is missing between them that keeps it from being a Testament as a whole for all sects. The two are actually born of each other. It was foretold that the events of the New Testament were to come, but the full comprehension of this knowledge was not clearly understood. Now, what we have is a division of understanding between the sects. Wars have been fought, people have been executed; in the name of God? No! It is the need to be right about something on one's own level.

God is absolute and wants us to understand the knowledge that we too are absolute, as part of the whole. Our little minds have a hard time accepting this truth, because we struggle within ourselves. One cannot have peace with others until one has peace within. There will always be a conflict in one way or another. For this reason we seek to find peace within ourselves. That is why it is written, "Know thyself."

Process

1. Write out an ego script of yourself.

2. Reverse the ego script to a Spirit mind script.

3. Write out how this feels.

The Five Stages of the Mind

An observation becomes a thought, then an emotion, to a sensation into manifestation.

O Observation
O Thought
O Emotion
O Sensation
O Manifestation

The larger the observation, the larger the thought that grows the emotion, enlarging the sensation, to enlargement of final manifestation. The smaller the observation the smaller the thought, shrinking the emotion that then shrinks the sensation, leading to a shrunken manifestation. In order to be fully present to your mind these need to be in complete alignment (size) with each other. Without the alignment (size) it becomes abstract and you do not know what you know, or how you feel or what you want. Your mind is out of alignment and each stage is working against one another, instead of in harmony with each other, which leads to a confused mind that acts and reacts automatically without full comprehension of what it is acting or reacting to.

If we add ego and Spirit we then have seven stages of the mind. The ideal plan is to take the five stages over to Spirit, realizing that it is all one mind at the present moment, and becoming fully aware of our conscious level of existence at any given moment. If it goes on auto pilot to the ego we are then at the mercy of where ego will place the five stages for the greater impact of going out of the moment and into the past or future, where the unconscious exists.

Why do I say that past or future would be unconscious? Because, to be in the present moment requires being conscious to your being. Unconscious and conscious cannot be simultaneously together at a present moment, one will cancel out the other. Therefore by learning the five stages of the mind we can better direct the five stages to the consciousness we desire.

Process

1. Bring a situation to mind, think about it for one minute.

2. Write out in detail the five stages of what you brought to mind and check to see if they are in alignment (size) with each other for full comprehension of the situation, making alignment adjustments where necessary.

3. Write out what your new aligned comprehension is about the situation.

Holy Trinity

The Holy Trinity is the power of Three; Father, Son and Holy Spirit. It is much like us, mind, body and spirit. When all three are connected on a conscious level there is certainty of the Law of Order, in which the universe exists.

We can also look at this as thought, feeling and action. All three need to be present in accordance with each other. If action takes over thought or feeling there becomes a quandary as to why you did something. You will find yourself saying, "I did it because I did and I don't know why I did." This is the case with automatic habits that we are unconscious to, like drinking too much or lighting that next cigarette etc. When in actuality our desires are not to over drink or maybe even not want to smoke at all, but the unconscious action takes over the thoughts and feelings. This also is a common theme that happens with people when feelings take over their thoughts. They may have a thought or a desired goal for themselves but their feelings are not in alignment with their thoughts, so you may have someone who says, "I want that desired goal but I'm feeling like it is too hard and uncomfortable and that gives me worry and fear about taking action." So begins another quandary in the mind.

The next quandary we will look at is thought, that is not in alignment with action. The thought is there but there seems to be a missing feeling. This could be in any area of one's life. Like, "I should love my spouse, or I think I have a good life, but I just can't seem to feel the love or the appreciation of my life." This then leads to actions of discontentment with a thought of leaving your spouse or looking elsewhere for a better life outside yourself, only to find where ever you go there you are. As you can see the quandary is always within the mind. This is what Holy Trinity is, a complete system of three. The Father and the Son are immersed in the Holy Spirit.

Three Centers

Thought
Feeling
Action

Use this method to get in touch with your present moment experiences. Check to see if they are in alignment, each doing their own job and not the others. By keeping them in proper order you will be well on your way to mastering your own mind and end the slavery of habitual behavior.

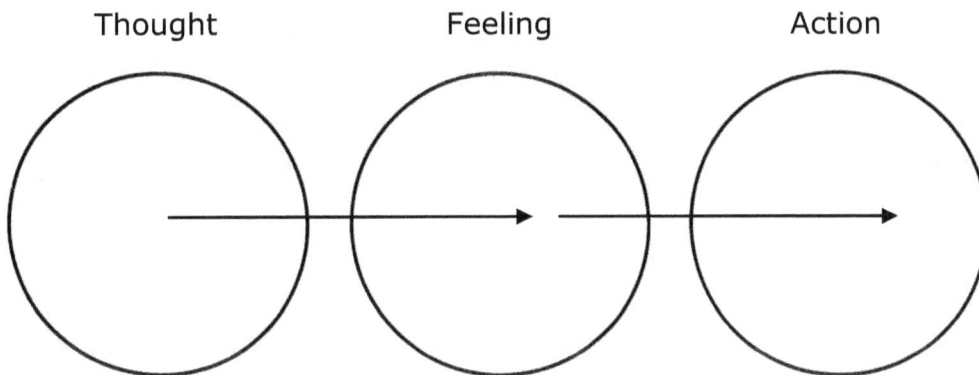

Thought   Feeling   Action

GOALS

Process

1. List your Spiritual goals.

2. Have your thoughts, feelings and actions be in alignment with your goals. Monitor yourself each day and write down your results.

3. Ask someone close to you if they have noticed a difference in your way of being. Write down their comments of noticed behavior.

Rome as the Center

During the time of the great Roman Empire it was Rome that built the roads that led to different destinations, utilizing Rome as the center. When it is said all roads lead to Rome, it is meant as a metaphor for centers of faith and knowledge that Spirit does not divide us but has us come to the same center through different roads for various lessons that are needed for our own personal growth in order to add to the whole of the universe. So, whatever road we are on is designed to lead us back to the center and if we should get confused all we need to do is remember where the location of the center is, just like travelers did if they became confused or lost. They knew finding Rome would bring them back to the center where they would know and recognize it as the center and to adjust or redirect their journey.

P.D. Ouspensky in his book: "In the Search of the Miraculous, The Teachings of G.I. Gurdjieff," wrote about it as in terms of intellectual, emotional and moving. I use the phrases thought, feeling and action when I work with clients. It doesn't matter what phrases are used to bring yourself back to the center of your mind. It is only important that you return to your center of knowing where you are going or coming from, as in the analogy of Rome as the center of faith and knowledge.

The center is the Holy Spirit. The journey is the right mind thinking and the wrong mind thinking. If you were to wake up in the morning with all kinds of thoughts of what you needed to accomplish within the day, it could become somewhat overwhelming, feeding into feelings of worry and fear or even failure of not completing each task. Your actions can become resentful and make the doing of the task a burden of your mental and physical activity; (Do you really desire this as your center for the day?) However, if you use the method of thought, feeling and action mindfully you can take each task and become fully engaged in it for the present moment you are in while doing it, so the thought of what you are doing complements the feeling of what you are doing and the action you are taking to have it started and completed to your own satisfaction before you move on to the next task. By doing this you are ending one journey to start on another. Each time you finish you move to the center for your next task. Wouldn't this be a much more desirable journey for your day?

Process

Using thought, feeling and actions:

1. Write out what needs to be done this week.

2. Record your daily thoughts, feelings and actions before and after each task. Make your recording brief so you can move on to the next task.

Keep in mind your desire to enjoy what you are doing while you are doing it!

Road of Emotional State

Our state of mind is something we need to control, if not our emotions become addicted to its behavior, and then our actions get addicted to the behavior. This all can become so automatic that we no longer feel we have control of our beingness and that outside forces are responsible for our actions. We sometimes fall unconsciously in love with these emotions and cling onto them, believing ourselves to be the emotions. We do this because we have not been taught how to properly harness the mind and lead it to the desired emotion, toward the desired action of what we truly want to experience.

If from an early age we were taught the mechanics of the two sides of one mind we could spare ourselves habits and addictions that do not serve us in what we are up to in life. For this reason I have always made it a point to teach my children how the mind works, so they are aware of emotional behaviors that could become addictions as to how they see themselves. It is never too early or too late to learn to manage the state of mind. The more resistance we encounter the more growth there is waiting for us to claim.

When we come to the fork in the road with the mind as to where to put a conscious thought there is the split mind to choose from, ego versus Spirit. We can place it in Spirit where there is peace and wholeness, but it is a conscious effort to keep thought from ego's automatic pilot system, until it becomes a non addictive behavior and transforms into a healthy automatic habit of the mind to find peace in Spirit mind thinking, leading to emotions that are desirable to one's actions of their beingness as whole and complete.

How long does this go on? From present moment to moment as long as we are in this classroom of life. In this continual beingness it becomes lighter and lighter to achieve.

Process

1. What ego addictions are you willing to give up and why?

2. What Spiritual habits do you want to keep practicing, put in or expand upon?

Super Conscious Mind and How It Works

Super conscious thoughts are when we go beyond what we consider our comfort zone. Take for instance, someone who is skilled in an area and does well enough to enjoy simple comforts, but only comforts, and sometimes goes into survival of those comforts and weaves back and forth between comfort and survival. They are living in what is called Mid Zone, the conscious mind of comfort and survival. The pitfalls of this mind thinking is that it can become very easy to fall from comfort into survival and when we are in survival we go into what is called the Low Zone area, where there is no room for dreams and aspirations that lead into the High Zone of super-conscious thoughts with super-conscious effort toward much more than mere survival and into a life of abundance in all areas.

Low zone is the area of lack, fear and scarcity over any given subject of your life. Nothing happens there. It is a place where one feels stuck and unable to move forward, where all old negative programs from the past are recorded and replayed.

That is why thinking in the super-conscious is so important. When one thinks in this realm and falls back they will still be thinking on a conscious level not in an unconscious level which is low zone behavior. The conscious mind can wake itself up to what the original dreams and aspirations are and move back up the ladder to that behavior once more. So, one is wavering back and forth from consciousness to super-consciousness instead of consciousness to unconsciousness, but to have this occur one must keep in mind super-conscious effort which is going beyond what is simply comfortable and moving above the imaginary perimeters. So, when the wavering comes into play you're still working between fully conscious and super-conscious.

Why do we waver back and forth? Because, that is the ebb and flow of life, ever changing like the seasons, the sun and the moon. We are not meant to stay the same, we are meant to evolve and create. If we do not we become stagnant and risk falling below our potential in the low zone.

Can someone remain in the high zone in all areas of life? It is difficult in a world of illusion to see ourselves as continuously mastering high zone behavior in all areas of life. We may have money handled but not relationships or physical body; such as weight and mental distress. So, it becomes a spinning act to keep all the plates spinning at the same time.

With the practice of expanding your consciousness to strive for super-conscious thoughts with super-conscious effort, you can achieve this from within the frame work of your Spiritual mind, because success is whatever you proclaim it to be for you. So, next time you feel you have just made a goal of comfort, push your consciousness to extra effort and keep your level of existence from falling below the conscious mid zone and back up to super-conscious high zone where dreams and aspirations are created and achieved.

Process

Examples of areas of life: Spiritual, Relationships, Career, Financial, Health/Fitness, Community, Education, etc.

1. What areas of your life are you in the low zone?

2. What areas of your life are you in the mid zone?

3. What areas of your life are you in the high zone?

4. Write out a plan for areas to be in the high zone and what super-conscious effort it will take to put them in action.

5. Write down what you're willing to give up and not willing to give up.

6. Write down what these goals and achievements will mean to you and what will be the new positive consequences in your life.

Process

Make a Mission Statement of your purpose in life using the "I am."

This is just an example, make your own mission statement and have fun with it. Keep it short so you can display and read it daily as your reminder of who you really are.

As in: "I am a powerful Spiritual being, who creates my desired goals that are important to me. I make a positive difference with the people I come in contact with. I strive to be the best I know how to be and continuously look for ways to grow in my knowledge of Spiritual awareness of myself. I respect and acknowledge the different modalities of humanities Spiritual search that comes from kindness and love. I hold no judgments as to who I think is right and who I think is wrong. I know that some of us are on the different roads going to the same destination and as we move forward we become sign posts for one another, leading the way to Universal Oneness."

Chapter 16

Twelve Months of Observation, Meditation and Application

How to use this section of the book.

Start and stay with one practice per month for the subconscious to absorb it fully into the mind body. It usually takes 28-30 days to program it into the body.

Our bodies have what is called fight or flight response. It operates on a subconscious level; like pumping blood, moving muscles and breathing air without being conscious of doing this, because it has been well trained to function this way from embryo. Once born into the world we begin to train it in other ways, either by modeling our caretakers or our observation of the world around us, always utilizing our fight or flight gauge, then storing that information within the subconscious mind in order to pull up the data at a later time to perceive as to fight or flight in any given mental or physical situation.

What we are attempting to do here is to retrain the subconscious body mind to fully observe, perceive and implement empowering results in your life.

I believe through these monthly practices you will have great results. I hope you will enjoy them as much as I enjoyed creating them for you.

How to use the Meditations

You will want to practice your meditations daily; morning is best to get your day started. You can memorize them or record them and play them for your own personal use when meditating. The idea is to have a quiet place where you will not be disturbed for the length of the meditation and to write down your received messages. The more you practice, the deeper your meditation will become. Never attempt to meditate while driving a vehicle or anytime your full attention is required, as meditation is a way to deeply relax the mind to receive messages from your subconscious mind to your super conscious mind, bringing you to a higher state of being. Enjoy and have fun with your inner wisdom. Allow yourself sacred time, which is the art of mindful nothingness, for even God rested on the seventh day and observed all He had accomplished. We as co-creators can do the same.

1 Monthly Practice

Faith

I want to expound upon the topic of Faith. Definition of faith: Believing in the unseen; that which is not yet here. Faith like everything else is a conversation, a conversation of expectation. When you operate from faith you are expecting the things you believe for, to come to you.

The opposite of faith is fear. Fear is also a conversation of expectation. The difference with fear from faith is with fear you are expecting not to get what you want, or expecting some terrible outcome to occur.

Again, because we magnetize to us our predominant thoughts and conversations, we need to have our thoughts and conversations in alignment to what we want, and not in alignment to what we don't want. We always want to think and speak in relation to what we want and not to what we don't want. We want to be speaking it "as if" it's already been manifested, "Calling those things that are not as if they were." Faith doesn't seem like it's natural for us. It seems we are "thrown to" fear more often than to faith. Faith is a learned behavior. In order for us to learn anything we need to practice it. If we practice the art of faith we will get good at faith. If we practice the art of fear we will get good at fear. What we want to get good at we need to practice! Why do we want to operate in faith rather than in fear? Because we are creators, with the power to create our outcomes and expectations. If we are expecting an outcome, we will manifest it. Our thoughts and conversations have the power to manifest the expected result. With the expectation of fear of an outcome not being what we want it to be, we can take the actions to manifest what we want, yet because of our predominant thought being fear we won't create our intended outcome through our actions. We will create the outcome we fear. That's how powerful our thoughts and conversations are. Therefore we need to operate in faith, expecting our outcome to be what we want it to be. Then, when we are taking actions to create what we want, our faith conversation will assist us in getting what we want with fewer struggles and more joy.

How do we operate in faith? By declaring with emotion that which we are committed to create, "as if" we've already created it. By instilling within ourselves the "belief" in the unseen goals we desire, then by taking actions consistently that will have us manifest our goals. By always telling ourselves that our goals are being manifested by our conscious mind we are then feeding it into the super-conscious mind. Faith then works through the super-conscious mind. The super-conscious mind wants you to have everything you tell it. That is why affirmations, prayer, and positive thoughts and conversations work toward the attainment of your goals.

Constantly feed yourself with faith filled thoughts, actions and motivational work, along with these monthly processes. Surround yourself with faith filled, motivated people. Keep the negative out, put the positive in. Take massive actions toward what you want and through your faith and your actions you will create it. You have the power to create whatever you want. Use your power, and enjoy the process of creating your goals, dreams, and desires. You deserve it!

Prayer: I give thanks and gratitude to faith in all areas of my life that the Divine Universal Strength which is in me will provide me and all humanity with divine wisdom to reach for faith in all matters of existence. Amen.

Affirmation: I lay it down and give it to my Higher Source which is universal faith in all I think and do.

Spiritual Meditation

Bring to mind a situation within you that you are working through. (pause) Once you have it in your mind get in a comfortable position and close your eyes, cleansing your mind of all thoughts and allowing a space for lightness and peace….. As you relax into this state you can feel a warm energy that relaxes you even more, dissolving away tension from your head…… down to your toes feeling deeply and deeply relaxed. Head relaxed, shoulders relaxed, chest more relaxed, abdomen very relaxed.   Breathe in from the belly out through the belly,….. Your hips are relaxed and legs deeply relaxed. You now feel a greater relaxation as your toes are relaxed….. You are now in a trance-state of deep relaxation. As you continue to breathe in through the belly out through the belly, you allow your mind to focus on a thought that you would like to heal within you while you are in this state of deep relaxation….. You are at peace and safe to be receptive now to go into even deeper meditation and visualization.

Take a deep breath through your nose in from your belly up to the top of your head. Hold to the count of 5 … Release it filling your belly back up with air and up to your head again, doing this 3 times, feeling a deeper sense of relaxation… Continue breathing in and out, in from the belly out through the belly… Now slowly count down from 7 to 1 each time going deeper, deeper and deeper, feeling very relaxed…

Now, imagine yourself in a small boat on a river floating along with the mountains on the right side of you, these mountains have wonderful formations. As you look up at the grey sky above you it begins to show signs of rain. As the grey clouds continue to appear you suddenly hear the sound of thunder and wild wind blowing though the trees from the left side of the river. As the rain begins to pour down you notice the river is taking the small boat downstream very rapidly. You now take 3 belly breaths in and out then counting down from 7… to 1… you relax even deeper, deeper and deeper, knowing that faith will keep you safe. As you look around, the wind stops blowing, the thunder has stopped and the river has become peaceful. You look up at the sky and the grey clouds part into a beautiful light blue sky with the sun beaming in. You look ahead and what you experience is a joyful, fun safe flow on the river. With a smile on your face you ask the question to the answer you want to know. Pause……………Be still and receive it. When you feel you are done, open your eyes and write down what you have received.

Insights from Meditation

Monthly Process

This month journal nightly on where you experience or practice faith each day. Write down at least 5 experiences when faith was present.

Nightly Journal Continued

#2 Monthly Practice

As A Man Thinketh

We're going to focus on a saying that you may have heard. "As a man thinketh in their heart, so are they also." There was also a book written by James Allen many years ago called: "As A Man Thinketh." I can't stress enough the importance of those words. This is a topic that will literally change your life when you understand and use it in the way that it can assist you in having what you want in your life.

Your thinking and your speaking control the outcomes of your life. Your destiny is in your words and thoughts. Today we're going to learn "how to" create your future the way you want it to be. By the way, your future can be one minute from now or years from now. You have the power to manifest it according to your thoughts and words, and then by the actions you take.

Each thought and word you create is taken into your subconscious mind as a truth. It doesn't know the difference between a lie and the truth. Because it accepts everything as a truth, it now has you work toward manifesting what you told it. Your super-conscious mind is your most powerful asset when you use it right. When it is used wrong it could be your most powerful detriment to your getting what you want.

Today we're going to learn how to make it work for us rather than against us. Left to it's own it will probably work against you. Why is that? I'll give you the reason I believe that's so. I believe that the majority of beings come out of childhood with so many more negative beliefs than positive beliefs. Especially beliefs about ourselves and what we are capable of. Because of that we are "thrown to" negative thoughts and conversations. Thoughts like: "It's going to be hard. I can't. I'm not enough. I'm afraid. I don't deserve it. It won't work. I might fail." etc. Remember, the theme of this practice is: "As a man thinketh in their heart, so are they also." So, if you're thinking all those negative thoughts you will create negative outcomes in your life. Whether we like it or not, that's the way it is. Therefore if you want a life with positive results you need to have thoughts and conversations that are also positive.

Because we are "thrown To" negative thoughts and conversations, the implementation of positive thoughts and conversations need to be done consciously and continuously. Just like you want positive results continuously, you need to speak and think positive continuously. Remember, "like attracts like."

How do you do that? By affirming what you want by your words and your thoughts, rather than what you have. Meaning, you have the power through your observations, thoughts, words, and actions to manifest what you want in your life, and yet a lot of times you may be speaking and thinking what you have. (negative or lack.) By speaking and thinking negative or lack you will create more negative or lack. By thinking and speaking and taking actions toward Positive, you will create positive results in your life. Make sense?

Don't think and speak about what you have, especially the negative. Think and speak about what you want, the positive results, and speak it "as if" you already have it. Use positive affirmations to cement what you want into your subconscious mind. Affirmations like: "I am healthy. I am joyful. Money flows to me freely. My life is easy and effortless. I deserve all good things. I believe in miracles and miracles occur for me," etc. These affirmations are "calling those things that are not "as if" they were."

Tell yourself positive empowering statements and conversations. Take consistent effective actions toward what you are declaring and you will have what you want. Use these techniques to enhance your life.

Prayer: I give thanks and gratitude for my positive thoughts that lead me into God's abundance where everything is possible. I know I am made in the eyes of the Great Creator and that I co-create with this Law of the Universe that brings me into wholeness. Amen.

Affirmation: I am a manifestation of all that I want. I keep my thoughts positive, for as a man thinketh, so he is.

Spiritual Meditation

Bring to mind a situation within you that you are working through. (Pause) Once you have it in your mind get in a comfortable position and close your eyes, cleansing your mind of all thoughts and allowing a space for lightness and peace….. As you relax into this state you can feel a warm energy that relaxes you even more, dissolving away tension from your head…… down to your toes feeling deeply and deeply relaxed. Head relaxed, shoulders relaxed, chest more relaxed, abdomen very relaxed. Breathe in from the belly out through the belly,….. Your hips are relaxed and legs deeply relaxed. You now feel a greater relaxation as your toes are relaxed….. You are now in a trance state of deep deep relaxation. As you continue to breathe in through the belly out through the belly, you allow your mind to focus on a thought that you would like to heal within you while you are in this state of deep relaxation….. You are at peace and safe to be receptive now to go into even deeper meditation and visualization.

Take a deep breath through your nose in from your belly up to the top of your head. Hold to the count of 5 … Release it filling your belly back up with air and up to your head again, doing this 3 times, feeling a deeper sense of relaxation… Continue breathing in and out, in from the belly out through the belly… Now slowly count down from 7 to 1 each time going deeper, deeper and deeper, feeling very relaxed…

Imagine yourself on top of a grassy hill overlooking the seashore. As you look further out to sea you notice a three masted schooner. As you continue to look out you notice the ship's crew are in long white robes with golden medallions hanging from their necks. You can see their white hair shining in the sun. There are three of them and they are waving you toward them. As you look down you see a green path leading down to the shore and you begin to walk down. As you reach the bottom you look up at the clouds above you and in an instance you know who the three crew members are. They are your guides coming to answer the three most important questions of your life. As you wait by the shoreline you prepare your questions about your situation. Pause......... The three guides are now approaching near the shore and with each step they are walking toward you to answer your three questions. Now ask each one for the answer you are seeking, for they are your own inner wisdom, manifested as the Holy Trinity in form. Now ask your questions and when you feel it is complete write down what comes to you.

Insights from Meditation

Monthly Process

Tell yourself positive empowering statements and conversations. Write down effective actions toward what you are declaring and record your results.

Continued Monthly Process

#3 Monthly Practice

The Law of Attraction

This month let's explore a "Law of the Universe." There are many Laws of the Universe and it's important for us to know them and then to work inside of them for our best results.

We have probably only been aware of the more popular laws like gravity. Gravity is certainly a good law to know for our survival. Such as if you step off the side of a ten story building you will fall. A good law to know. Yet, there are so many others that perhaps won't interfere with our survival, yet will enhance our lives and the lives of others.

The law we will explore today is the Law of Attraction. Let's use this law for the attainment of our goals. First off let's define what I mean by the universe. The universe for these examples is everything outside of us. Everything you can see and everything you can't see.

The law of attraction is a law that's in effect whether we like it or not. Such as all the other laws of the universe. The purpose of our becoming familiar with the laws is to use them to our advantage, rather than having them be used to our disadvantage. Today we are going to get literate with the law of attraction.

The law of attraction simply stated is: Like attracts like. What we are manifesting within us will be manifested outside of us. Such as if we're manifesting negative thoughts and conversations within we will attract negative outcomes. If we're manifesting positive thoughts and conversations within we will attract positive results in our universe. Pretty simple isn't it? Perhaps not easy, yet simple. What will make it easy is when you practice it over and over again. We are always practicing something. That something could be for our good or it could be for our detriment. We want to make sure we are practicing things and habits for our good.

How can we use the law of attraction for our good? First we want to decide what we want to attract. Do we want to attract something negative into our space or something positive? Whatever we want to attract we need to manifest those same type thoughts and conversations within us constantly and consistently. In order to do that we need to become conscious to our every thought, conversation, and feeling. It is estimated that we speak somewhere between 300-800 words per minute every waking hour, either out loud or in our

190

thoughts. A lot of our speaking and thinking is unconscious to us. It's like we're on automatic and the thoughts and conversations just come. We need to get in control of those conversations and thoughts and have each of them be in alignment to what we want to manifest in our Universe. The way to do that is to always speak and think positive empowering words. When you don't, change it to positive before you have completed the statement or thought. If you've completed the negative thought or conversation, tell yourself "cancel cancel" and restate the thought or conversation to be positive. By consistently having positive and empowering thoughts and conversations, along with taking positive powerful actions, you will manifest powerful positive results in your universe. Make sense?

This law also works for other areas you want to manifest in your life. If you want love you need to give love. If you want respect you need to give respect. If you want friendliness you need to give friendliness. If you want money you need to give Money. If you want peace you need to give peace. If you want time you need to give time, etc. Whatever you want from without you need to first manifest from within.

There you have it. The law of attraction. It can work for you or it can work against you. You have the choice and the power to choose for or against. Choose for and let the universe be your friend and ally in accomplishing your goals, dreams, and desires.

Monthly Process

1. List areas of your life that you want to change.

2. List what you want to attract in these areas.

3. Write out action steps you need to adjust or take to attract that which you want.

4. Record your results.

Prayer: I give thanks and gratitude for mirroring Spirit's love, forgiveness and peace of Universal Oneness and that it is reflected back to me by my actions through faith and inner peace. Amen.

Affirmation: I attract all that is of love, forgiveness, peace and joy. I am a natural magnet of Spirit and it is mirrored back to me through my thoughts.

Spiritual Meditation

Bring to mind a situation within you that you are working through. (Pause) Once you have it in your mind get in a comfortable position and close your eyes, cleansing your mind of all thoughts and allowing a space for lightness and peace….. As you relax into this state you can feel a warm energy that relaxes you even more, dissolving away tension from your head…… down to your toes feeling deeply and deeply relaxed. Head relaxed, shoulders relaxed, chest more relaxed, abdomen very relaxed.   Breathe in from the belly out through the belly,….. your hips are relaxed and legs deeply relaxed. You now feel a greater relaxation as your toes are relaxed….. You are now in a trance- state of deep deep relaxation. As you continue to breathe in through the belly out through the belly, you allow your mind to focus on a thought that you would like to heal within you while you are in this state of deep relaxation….. You are at peace and safe to be receptive now to go into even deeper meditation and visualization.

Take a deep breath through your nose in from your belly up to the top of your head. Hold to the count of 5 … Release it filling your belly back up with air and up to your head again, doing this 3 times, feeling a deeper sense of relaxation… Continue breathing in and out, in from the belly out through the belly… Now slowly count down from 7 to 1 each time going deeper, deeper and deeper, feeling very relaxed…

Imagine walking on a sandy beach with the sound of white capped waves moving forward toward the sand. As you look down at your feet they become covered with warm bright blue sea water and tiny little white bubbles of sea caps. With a sense of peace and relaxation you smell the freshness of the sea and hear the musical sound of seagulls flying above you. As you look up you see the clouds part and expose a radiant rainbow that uses the water as a reflection of its beauty. You take in this moment with peace and relaxing and in your thoughts you

ask Spirit within for the answer you want to know. Pause...........................
As you remain in this deep, deep deep sense of relaxation you listen
and receive the answer. Without judgment or analyzing it you repeat it
out loud. When you feel it is complete you open your eyes and begin to
write down what you have received.

Insights from Meditation

#4 Monthly Practice

Positive Attitude

Let's explore the concepts of attitude and altitude. In this case "Your attitude determines your altitude." First let's look at what we mean when we speak of attitude. Your attitude is where you operate from; Your predominant thoughts and conversations. How you see something or envision something, either in the past, the present, or the future. How you see yourself and your abilities. Your attitude is "made up" by you. Now, it may have been shaped by your experiences in your life, or by what evidence you've used to create your attitude, but it is "made up," using whatever information you choose to use. Once it's "made up" you will then find more evidence to be right about why your attitude is correct.

We Spiritual beings on a human journey are right machines. We create something in our mind and then go out to collect the evidence to support our being right. It's kind of an unwritten "law of the universe." It coincides with the "law of attraction." Like attracts like; Meaning, that if your attitude is predominately negative you will attract negative results in your life. If your attitude is predominately positive you will attract positive results in your life. The eastern Religions and philosophies call this karma. Psychics say: Every action creates a subsequent reaction. The Christian Religion says: If you <u>believe</u> and say to the mountain move, the mountain will move. Modern philosophers say: Whatever the mind can <u>believe</u> and <u>conceive</u> it will achieve. However it is said it all comes down to the same thing, "like attracts like!"

That's what is meant by, Your attitude determines your altitude; altitude being how high you will go in life. If you have a negative attitude you can expect to have negative results in your life. You may not like that fact, yet it is the way that it is. As with all the "laws of the universe", you may not like them yet they still exist as they are, whether you like them or not. Therefore because they are, you need to learn them and then live "inside" those laws to make them work for you and what you are up to in life.

The law of attraction (like attracts like) means that you have to have a positive attitude if you want to attract positive results. Again, how do we determine if an attitude or thought is positive or negative? If it isn't lining up with what we want, it's negative; If it's lining up with what we want it's positive. Because we make up our thoughts and attitudes, we need to make sure they are consistent with what we want in our life and if they're not we <u>need</u> to change them so that they are. That means we need to continuously speak and think into existence, in the present moment, the future we want to attain, and we need to speak and think it "as if" it's already here. (positive affirmations) We then need to take actions consistent with what we want, and we will attain what we want more often then not.

It's that simple; easy no, simple yes. What makes a simple process easy is when we continuously practice the simple process. Start practicing talking, thinking, believing that which you want in life is already here. Start practicing taking massive actions toward that which you want in life and you will <u>attract</u> to you that which you want. Continuously work on your attitude. Call yourself up to be operating from a spirit of play, a positive attitude, and empowering conversations to yourself and others, and have fun taking the actions to get there. When you consistently operate from a positive attitude your goals, dreams, and desires will be realized with more ease and less effort. You deserve the life you want, now go out and create it!

Monthly Process

Make a list of your goals, dreams and desires. List all action steps needed to manifest them. Check your action steps daily and check off each of your accomplishments for the next 30 days.

Continued Monthly Process

Prayer: Spirit mind guide me through my daily thoughts. Guide me to a positive loving attitude that will bring me to my highest altitude. For this I give gratitude. Amen.

Affirmation: I know I create my mental state by my attitude, so I use Spirit mind to guide me to my highest good.

Spiritual Meditation

Bring to mind a situation within you that you are working through. (Pause) Once you have it in your mind get in a comfortable position and close your eyes, cleansing your mind of all thoughts and allowing a space for lightness and peace….. As you relax into this state you can feel a warm energy that relaxes you even more, dissolving away tension from your head…… down to your toes feeling deeply and deeply relaxed. Head relaxed, shoulders relaxed, chest more relaxed, abdomen very relaxed. Breathe in from the belly out through the belly,….. your hips are relaxed and legs deeply relaxed. You now feel a greater relaxation as your toes are relaxed….. You are now in a trance-state of deep deep relaxation. As you continue to breathe in through the belly out through the belly, you allow your mind to focus on a thought that you would like to heal within you while you are in this state of deep relaxation….. You are at peace and safe to be receptive now to go into even deeper meditation and visualization.

Take a deep breath through your nose in from your belly up to the top of your head. Hold to the count of 5 … Release it filling your belly back up with air and up to your head again, doing this 3 times, feeling a deeper sense of relaxation… Continue breathing in and out, in from the belly out through the belly… Now slowly count down from 7 to 1 each time going deeper, deeper and deeper, feeling very relaxed…

Imagine yourself on a high mountain top sitting in a lotus position. As you look around you see beautiful red colored mountains. One is shaped like a bell tower; the other is shaped like the head of an Indian chief. All around you see peaks and valleys of beautiful formed mountains, each resembling a different formation of familiarity. As you touch your index finger to your thumb you look up to see the most radiant orange colored clouds with the sun setting behind them illuminating them with yellow colored clouds as well. In this place of peace and deep, deep deep relaxation your inner Spirit will answer the question you are looking for. Pause......................... As you remain in this quiet bliss and positive attitude you listen for the answer from Spirit within and repeat it out loud without judgment or analyzing it. When you feel complete open your eyes and write down what you have received.

Insights from Meditation

#5 Monthly Practice

Living in the Present Moment

Where is your future created? In the present moment! Whatever you're doing or not doing now will directly affect your future. Does that make sense? For example, if you want to weigh a certain weight in six months (your future), you need to take consistent actions now (your present), to manifest the certain weight you want to achieve. You need to exercise now. You need to eat right now. You need to live a balanced life now to have your future weight be what you want it to be. The same goes with every area of your life. Your financial future. Your spiritual future. Your relationship future. Your health/fitness future. Whatever area(s) of your life you want to be different in your future you need to design and take actions now.

What is it you want in six months, one year, two years, etc? Write out what it is you want and by when you want it. Then write out all the actions it will take to have you achieve what you want. Again, not just the actions you want to take, the actions it will take to achieve it. At this point it's crucial for you to schedule your actions in your planner. By the way, if you're not using a planner this is a great time to start. It is a devise that will make sure nothing falls through the cracks, and that you are regimented in your action steps, and that you are consistent in what needs doing. Remember your future will get here whether you take the appropriate actions or not. The only difference is, if you take the actions your future will be more in line with what you want. If you don't take the actions consistent with what you want, your future will just be "more of the same." Six months, one year, two years will get here either way. Your job is to have it be how you want it to be.

Each week plan out your schedule and make sure you list the things that you need to do in alignment with what you want your future to be. When the scheduled time comes to take the action make sure you take the action. You might want to talk yourself out of taking the action. Thoughts may come to you like: "I'm too busy to do this right now. This will be hard. I'm not sure I can do this. What if this or that happens? I'll just put it off until tomorrow," etc. No matter what the thoughts you create to talk yourself out of the action, you need to take the action.

"Just do it!" Even though you think you're not enough, just do it. Even though you might want to put it off, just do it. Keep practicing just doing it, even when you don't want to just do it and you will get good at just doing it. Keep practicing putting off just doing it and you will get good at putting off just doing it. Whatever you practice you get good at. Keep practicing the actions that will have you create the future you want, and when your future gets here it will be the one you planned for, acted upon, and created. You deserve it, start it now!

Monthly Process

Write down positive statements about your goals using "I am." "I am successful. I am in a great relationship," etc. Speak it as if it's already happened. Keep a small card in your wallet, on your phone or computer with your goals written out and action steps needed. Record your daily results.

Continued Monthly Process

Prayer: I give thanks and relax in perfect oneness with the moment that is. Spirit guides my mind to right minded thinking for myself and all humanity, and because of that Grace I am a whole and complete Spiritual creation at one with the universe. Amen.

Affirmation: I am a Spiritual being on a human journey living fully in the present moment that then creates my future according to the action steps I have taken at the present moment.

Spiritual Meditation

Bring to mind a situation within you that you are working through. (Pause) Once you have it in your mind get in a comfortable position and close your eyes, cleansing your mind of all thoughts and allowing a space for lightness and peace….. As you relax into this state you can feel a warm energy that relaxes you even more, dissolving away tension from your head…… down to your toes feeling deeply and deeply relaxed. Head relaxed, shoulders relaxed, chest more relaxed, abdomen very relaxed. Breathe in from the belly out through the belly,….. your hips are relaxed and legs deeply relaxed. You now feel a greater relaxation as your toes are relaxed….. You are now in a trance state of deep deep relaxation. As you continue to breathe in through the belly out through the belly, you allow your mind to focus on a thought that you would like to heal within you while you are in this state of deep relaxation….. You are at peace and safe to be receptive now to go into even deeper meditation and visualization.

Take a deep breath through your nose in from your belly up to the top of your head. Hold to the count of 5 … Release it filling your belly back up with air and up to your head again, doing this 3 times, feeling a deeper sense of relaxation… Continue breathing in and out, in from the belly out through the belly… Now slowly count down from 7 to 1 each time going deeper, deeper and deeper, feeling very relaxed…

Imagine yourself walking onto a bridge overlooking a beautiful stream and seeing a bright sun coming from behind the clouds engulfing everything around you into a soft warm spring day, where you can smell the scent of jasmine and notice the large trees around you. As you inhale the smell of fresh jasmine you feel a sense of knowingness and in this sense of knowingness you become even more relaxed and peaceful. As you approach the end of the bridge there is a Spirit guide awaiting you with their hand stretched out. As you take the hand you recognize it as your inner knowingness. You ask the question to what you want to know. Then in this place of peace you allow the answer to come to the surface without judgment or analyzing. You just allow the present moment to take place and repeat out loud the answer you are receiving. Stay relaxed and at peace. When you feel it is complete open your eyes and write down what you have received.

Insights from Meditation

#6 Monthly Practice

Commitment

Let's explore the concept called Commitment. Definition of commitment (mine): Doing what you said you would do even after the excitement of having said it has worn off. Commitment has nothing to do with feelings. What I mean by that is, once you've committed to something you may not "feel" like doing it when the appointed time comes to do it. You may not "feel" like getting up in the morning when the alarm goes off. You may not "feel" like exercising when you said you would. You may not "feel" like making prospecting calls when you said you would. You may not "feel" like doing the chores you committed to, etc. Your feelings don't matter. Not that you don't matter, but your feelings don't matter. What matters is your initial commitment. That's what we need to use to drive us, our initial commitment, not our feelings. Our commitments are solid and steady; our feelings will take us all over the place. Sometimes we feel tired. Sometimes we feel scared. Sometimes we feel lazy. Sometimes we feel like avoiding, or putting things off (procrastinating) etc. If we let our feelings run us, we will be all over the place regarding our actions toward our commitments. When we operate from our commitments, our actions will be consistent with our commitments or goals, thereby taking more actions to realize our initial commitment. More actions create more results.

How can you operate from your commitments on a consistent basis? By first declaring what your commitments are in each area of your life; financial, spiritual, relationship, career, education, health/fitness, community, etc. By knowing what you want and being willing to commit to it, then becomes your guiding light as to where you want to get to. It will be a consistent place to operate from and a consistent place you are committed to get to.

Once you've declared your commitments you need to define the actions you need to take to get there. Not the actions you "feel "like taking, the actions you need to take that are in alignment with your getting there. Then when the scheduled time to take the action is at hand you need to start taking the actions. Remember, what stops most people is the start. Once you start taking the actions the battle over

207

your feelings is 75 % won. We Spiritual beings were created to create. We weren't created to sit around wishing and hoping that we can have our goals. We were created to have the ability to imagine our goals, commit to our goals, and to take the actions to manifest our goals. (Notice how much more energy and enthusiasm you have when you're in action then when you're sitting around wishing and hoping your life were different.) Your feelings are usually the reason why you don't do what you know you need to do. Be driven and guided by your commitments and observe how your feelings will line up with your commitments. Start now!

Monthly Process

Write down your commitments in all areas of your life. Declare and write down the actions you will take. Schedule the actions on a consistent basis. Then, when the scheduled time comes to take the action; take the action. Live your life based on your commitments and this method and you will have the life you love. That's your birthright; claim it. Record your results.

Continued Monthly Process

Prayer: I give thanks and gratitude to Spirit, Who is always with me and always, supports me in the positive things I am committed to and that gives me the strength to take the actions in which I declare is needed for the desire. Amen.

Affirmation: I am committed to the things I declare that I want. I am committed to take action toward those things in which I declare and desire.

Spiritual Meditation

Bring to mind a situation within you that you are working through. (Pause) Once you have it in your mind get in a comfortable position and close your eyes, cleansing your mind of all thoughts and allowing a space for lightness and peace….. As you relax into this state you can feel a warm energy that relaxes you even more, dissolving away tension from your head…… down to your toes feeling deeply and deeply relaxed. Head relaxed, shoulders relaxed, chest more relaxed, abdomen very relaxed.   Breathe in from the belly out through the belly,….. your hips are relaxed and legs deeply relaxed. You now feel a greater relaxation as your toes are relaxed….. You are now in a trance state of deep deep relaxation. As you continue to breathe in through the belly out through the belly, you allow your mind to focus on the situation that you would like to heal while you are in this state of deep relaxation….. You are at peace and safe to be receptive now to go into even deeper meditation and visualization.

Take a deep breath through your nose in from your belly up to the top of your head. Hold to the count of 5 … Release it filling your belly back up with air and up to your head again, doing this 3 times, feeling a deeper sense of relaxation… Continue breathing in and out, in from the belly out through the belly… Now slowly count down from 7 to 1 each time going deeper, deeper and deeper, feeling very relaxed…

Imagine yourself walking on a path in the woods on a very early morning, stepping on foliage colored leaves and hearing their crackling sound as you take each step. You can also hear the woodpeckers in the trees, and as you look up at the morning clouds they begin to part. Through the trees you see a bright sun rising, illuminating the whole forest, turning it into a beautiful bright sanctuary in which you feel at peace. You then see a large red log on which you seat yourself with palms open to receive. You ask for the answer to your question to be put in the palms of your hand. Within seconds you receive a golden scroll in which your answer is written. As you hold onto this scroll, relax and ask your question and as you ask it you can feel the answer being received through your palms into your mind. When you feel it is complete, write down what you have received.

Insights from Meditation

#7 Monthly Practice

Confidence and Certainty

This month I'd like to explore the concepts of Confidence and Certainty. Let's put a definition to the word confidence. Confidence is a knowing that you are capable and have the ability to handle a particular situation, or create a goal you've declared. Certainty is a sureness that you are capable and able to handle the situations that arise in life. Certainty is not ego or pride. It is a knowingness regarding your power and ability to accomplish.

What is the opposite of certainty? Doubt. Doubt in your abilities. Doubt that the outcome will not be what you desire. When certainty goes away doubt comes in. A good way to check in with yourself regarding where you are operating from is to check your results. If you don't have the results you want most likely doubt has crept in, and if you are attaining your goals certainty is probably present. Not that you are attaining your goals and certainty occurs. It is that you are coming from certainty and then creating your goals.

Doubt and certainty are ways of being, not something to do. Again, a way of being is the conversation or declaration you are coming from. Your way of being is much more important than what you are doing. That's why we're called human being and not human doing.

Doubt is a way of being, just as certainty is a way of being. Coming from certainty increases your confidence, which in turn increases your attitude, which in turn increases your actions and your effectiveness, which in turn increases your results. Make sense? Coming from doubt reduces your confidence, which in turn reduces your attitude, which in turn reduces your actions and effectiveness, which in turn reduces your results. All that being said, doesn't it make sense for you to "come from" certainty in all areas of your life? Even if consciously you don't believe it at 100%. You still can come from certainty.

How do you do that? How do you convince yourself to come from certainty? First off you need to declare it to yourself; in your speaking and especially in your thoughts. Whenever a doubt conversation or thought starts to creep in, you need to change it to a certainty conversation. In all situations you need to declare: "I don't know what it will look like but I'll........" The.......... being whatever you want to manifest.

Secondly, you need to surround yourself with people who believe in you and who champion you rather than the nay-sayers or people who continuously put you or your dreams down. You need to focus on the positives of life rather than the negatives of life. (What you look for you will find!)

Most importantly, you need to stay in effective actions toward your goals, along with declaring effective conversations about the attainment of your goals; Continuously making yourself believe it even before you see it.

You've probably lived long enough to observe that illusionary life goes up and down. Sometimes things turn out the way you want them to and sometimes they don't. That life goes up and down is a given and we can't change that. What we can change is our conversation or way of being. It can remain constant. We can continuously come from certainty and confidence. We are in charge of our conversations (thoughts). So, we are in charge of our way of being. Staying conscious to a conversation of certainty is a way to keep certainty present. Continuously speak to yourself in certainty conversations, statements, and thoughts. Continuously look for the good in your life and in every situation. Continuously take effective actions toward your goals.

Continuously enjoy the process called life. Expect miracles to occur in your life and miracles will occur. Definition of miracles: Something that wasn't going to happen ordinarily. You deserve the best, now go and create it!

Monthly Process

List the areas that you would like to have more confidence and thoughts of certainty. Examine them well and write out what it would take to be confident and certain in these areas, then take action each day on what you have written. At the end of the day write down at least 5 experiences that you had confidence and certainty in.

Continued Monthly Process

Prayer: I give thanks and gratitude to the absolute oneness of all that is and know that as part of that oneness all prayers are received as one consciousness of thought, and for this I have confidence and certainty in all that I am.

Affirmation: I have confidence and certainty in all my thoughts, by taking them away from ego and placing them with Spirit.

Spiritual Meditation

Bring to mind a situation within you that you are working through. (Pause) Once you have it in your mind get in a comfortable position and close your eyes, cleansing your mind of all thoughts and allowing a space for lightness and peace..... As you relax into this state you can feel a warm energy that relaxes you even more, dissolving away tension from your head...... down to your toes feeling deeply and deeply relaxed. Head relaxed, shoulders relaxed, chest more relaxed, abdomen very relaxed. Breathe in from the belly out through the belly,..... your hips are relaxed and legs deeply relaxed. You now feel a greater relaxation as your toes are relaxed..... You are now in a trance-state of deep deep relaxation. As you continue to breathe in through the belly out through the belly, you allow your mind to focus on a situation that you would like to heal within you while you are in this state of deep relaxation..... You are at peace and safe to be receptive now to go into even deeper meditation and visualization.

Take a deep breath through your nose in from your belly up to the top of your head. Hold to the count of 5 ... Release it filling your belly back up with air and up to your head again, doing this 3 times, feeling a deeper sense of relaxation... Continue breathing in and out, in from the belly out through the belly... Now slowly count down from 7 to 1 each time going deeper, deeper and deeper, feeling very relaxed...

Now bring to mind the areas in which you desire more confidence and certainty. Imagine you are walking on a path toward a large grassy mountain top where there are people gathered all around. As you walk up the path there is a soft breeze blowing with just the right amount of warmth on your face. You look up just in time to see some white clouds part and expose the beauty of the sun and the smell of sage in the air. As you continue to walk toward the crowd of people you notice that you know everyone there and that they know you. They have been awaiting your arrival. As you look at each face you recognize them as family, friends, and acquaintances. Out from the crowd comes forth a person you recognize as your Spirit guide, someone who has always been there for you and now you are there on the grassy mountain top to deliver a message of love given to you from your Spirit guide that you have worked so closely with from within. As you look around you hear questions from the crowd. One at a time, looking at the face that is asking the question you answer with confidence and certainty as to why they are in your life and what you have to offer by being in their life. Stay relaxed and allow it to flow. Now, ask your Spirit guide for the answer to the situation you are working through. When you feel it is complete, write what you have received.

Insights from Meditation

#8 Monthly Practice

Responsibility of Cause and Effect

This month I want to talk about the aspect of Responsibility. For the purpose of this conversation let's define the word responsibility. Responsibility has been said to be the willingness to experience yourself as cause in the matter. It's not guilt, blame, shame, fault, burden, or any other negative meanings you may have given to it. Even though that's how some of us were raised to believe. You were responsible to do your homework, almost like a burden. You were responsible to do good and if you didn't you felt guilty or the thought that guilt was being put upon you. So it was almost like; "Don't give me any more responsibility it's too much like burden". None of that is responsibility. Responsibility is coming from being cause in the matter.

The opposite of cause in the matter is the effect of the matter. When you operate from the effect of the matter you give up your power to the matter or you become victim to the matter. The matter being those things in your life such as: Money, time, the economy, family, health/fitness, friends, the weather, traffic, etc. When you come from cause in the matter you have power over the matter.

As it has been stated: "If it's to be it's up to me!" That is cause in the matter. What it is saying is that whatever is going on or whatever I want, it's up to me to get it, or create it, or be it. Can you see the power that comes from operating like that? Rather than coming from the place of: They did it to me, or I can't do this or that, or I don't know what to do, or there's nothing I can do, etc.

When you operate (declare) coming from cause in the matter it opens up so many more possibilities for you to do and create. When you operate from the effect (victim) to the matter it closes down your possibilities because you won't be able to see them.

I've heard people say things like: "It didn't work out. He or she hurt my feelings. Life is hard. The market is slow, etc." Like all these things and occurrences are outside of you and you have no power over them. The good news is they are not because when you come from cause in the matter (If it's to be it's up to me) you have access and the power to change those things in your life that may not be to your liking, to having them the way you want them. Coming from cause you will see what you can do to change them. Coming from the effect (victim) you won't see what you can do to change them because you'll probably be saying: "It's not my fault. There's nothing I can do. I'll just have to wait till it turns around, etc." Make sense?

This month look at those areas you want to improve or enhance. Declare your being cause in the matter (If it's to be it's up to me) Then from that place write down the action steps you will take this month in order to have what you say you want! Take the action steps coming from total cause in the matter and watch how your energy level will increase, your creativity will be enhanced, your joy will grow, and you will be making things happen rather than waiting for them to happen.

Monthly Process:

1. List what responsibilities you are not taking action on and where you see yourself as the effect instead of the cause.

2. Write down the responsible action steps you need to take to create what you declare you want to cause.

Prayer: I give thanks and gratitude to the Universal light of all that is; because I know within the thoughts of responsibility I can create great causation and effect of love with all that I do and all I come in contact with. Thank you Spirit. Amen.

Affirmation: I am responsible for all my actions in order to receive my desired effects as cause in the matter.

Spiritual Meditation

Bring to mind a situation within you that you are working through. (Pause) Once you have it in your mind get in a comfortable position and close your eyes, cleansing your mind of all thoughts and allowing a space for lightness and peace….. As you relax into this state you can feel a warm energy that relaxes you even more, dissolving away tension from your head…… down to your toes feeling deeply and deeply relaxed. Head relaxed, shoulders relaxed, chest more relaxed, abdomen very relaxed. Breathe in from the belly out through the belly,….. your hips are relaxed and legs deeply relaxed. You now feel a greater relaxation as your toes are relaxed….. You are now in a trance-state of deep deep relaxation. As you continue to breathe in through the belly out through the belly, you allow your mind to focus on a thought that you would like to heal within you while you are in this state of deep relaxation….. You are at peace and safe to be receptive now to go into even deeper meditation and visualization.

Take a deep breath through your nose in from your belly up to the top of your head. Hold to the count of 5 … Release it filling your belly back up with air and up to your head again, doing this 3 times, feeling a deeper sense of relaxation… Continue breathing in and out, in from the belly out through the belly… Now slowly count down from 7 to 1 each time going deeper, deeper and deeper, feeling very relaxed…

Now imagine yourself in a slight mist on a cobble stoned street with very old buildings all lined up side by side. There is a row of small stores with large windows. As you look through each window you see your reflection, and beyond that you create inside each store what you would like to create and see within yourself. As you approach each window take a deep breath 3 times up from the belly down through the belly. Allow yourself to take responsibility for what you cause in each store and take notice as to the effect it has on you. Keep going from store window to store window. When you have reached the end take a

222

deep belly breath 3 more times and relax, counting down from 7 to 1, relax deeper, deeper and deeper. Now ask yourself what you created in each window as your inner self beyond your reflection. When you are ready open your eyes and write down what you saw.

Insights from Meditation

#9 Monthly Practice

The Art of Inner Happiness

This month let's talk about fun and joy. From where could one create fun and joy? At an amusement park? On vacation? At the beach? At a party? etc. No, not from any of these places. Where fun and joy, for that matter any emotion, is created is within you. Not outside of you. What do I mean by within you? In your observations, thoughts and conversations. Oh no you say, not my observations, thoughts and conversations again. Yes, your observations, thoughts and conversations. That is where everything you experience outside of you first takes place. For example: Vacations are advertised to "be relaxing and happy," or something like that. Yet, when I see people on vacation I don't see all the people there being relaxed and happy. They may be complaining about the costs. They may be complaining about the long lines at the airport. They may be complaining about the cost of food. They may be complaining about the hotel. etc. If happiness were created from outside of us, all we'd have to do is find a happy vacation place and then we'd be happy. Not so.

Where we need to look for that happy place is within us. Joy within will create happiness outside. It just doesn't happen though; we need to work at it. We need to constantly fill our observations, thoughts and conversations with joyful material. You need to observe the joy in your life. You need to observe conversations and thoughts of joy.

There are two ways you can observe your life, joyful or burdensome. You have the power to choose either one. Things to do in your life can be either a "have to" or a "get to." I "have to" get up this morning, or I "get to" get up this morning. I "have to" make these phone calls, or I "get to" make these phone calls. I "have to" be nice to my spouse, or I "get to" be nice to my spouse. I "have to" go to work, or I "get to" go to work, etc. A "have to" life creates a burdensome life. A "get to" life creates a joyful life.

You have the choice of how you can create your life by "where you come from." Not where you come from like Buffalo, New York, where you "come from" regarding how you declare your life to be. Come from is where you operate from. Your core observations and conversations. Your way of being. You create a "come from" by what you consistently tell yourself. Joy is a "come from." You create joy by consistently observing joyful thoughts and conversations. In order to have a joyful life on a consistent basis you need to observe joyful thoughts and conversations on a consistent basis. When you sow joyful thoughts and conversations you will Reap joy in your life. When you sow negative burdensome thoughts and conversations you will reap a negative burdensome life. Whatever you want to reap, you first have to sow.

How do I do that when I don't "feel" my life is joyful? By creating observations of joy and abundance and constantly stating them, with feeling, out loud and in your mind. You will then observe the evidence of joy everywhere you look.

Question: From where could someone create happiness?

Answer: From within one's own mind.

Monthly Process

1. Make a list of things that bring happiness and fun to your life. Check in and see how many of those things come from within.

2. At the end of each day write down at least 5 happy experiences that came from within.

Continued Monthly Process

Prayer: I give thanks and gratitude for all the happiness and fun I'm able to create within myself, through the Great Creator that You God have provided to me through my thoughts. Amen.

Affirmation: I make my experience of life happy and fun by the thoughts that come from within me.

Spiritual Meditation

Bring to mind a situation within you that you are working through. (Pause) Once you have it in your mind get in a comfortable position and close your eyes, cleansing your mind of all thoughts and allowing a space for lightness and peace..... As you relax into this state you can feel a warm energy that relaxes you even more, dissolving away tension from your head...... down to your toes feeling deeply and deeply relaxed. Head relaxed, shoulders relaxed, chest more relaxed, abdomen very relaxed. Breathe in from the belly out through the belly,..... your hips are relaxed and legs deeply relaxed. You now feel a greater relaxation as your toes are relaxed..... You are now in a trance-state of deep deep relaxation. As you continue to breathe in through the belly out through the belly, you allow your mind to focus on a thought that you would like to heal within you while you are in this state of deep relaxation..... You are at peace and safe to be receptive now to go into even deeper meditation and visualization.

Take a deep breath through your nose in from your belly up to the top of your head. Hold to the count of 5 ... Release it filling your belly back up with air and up to your head again, doing this 3 times, feeling a deeper sense of relaxation... Continue breathing in and out, in from the belly out through the belly... Now slowly count down from 7 to 1 each time going deeper, deeper and deeper, feeling very relaxed...

Imagine yourself in the middle of a jungle where you can hear the sounds of roaming animals. They are tamed and gentle as you are creating them through your thoughts. As you walk on a path through this jungle you hear monkeys laughing in the trees and swinging playfully from branch to branch. As you look up at these large trees you see the clouds in the sky with the sun peaking through the trees. You feel happy and playful knowing that your thoughts are creating this for you. As you continue to walk the path you hear a pleasant sound of laughter. You follow that sound until you find a beautiful giant waterfall flowing into a pool of water with the most radiant rainbow running across it. You take a deep belly breath 3 times and count down from 7 to 1 going deeper and deeper into relaxation. Now that you are deeply relaxed you see where the laughter is coming from. It is your inner child, the All knowing you laughing with your playful thoughts from within. As you connect with yourself you ask questions about your own inner happiness and what you need to do to have happiness and fun from within. Listen and when you feel it is complete open your eyes and write down what you have received.

Insights from Meditation

#10 Monthly Practice

Karma

Have you ever heard the word Karma? Karma basically means: What you put out in the universe comes back to you. The universe being everything outside of you. It can be explained in a lot of different ways. Like attracts like. What you sow you reap. Be careful what you wish for, you just might get it. What the mind can believe and conceive it can achieve. The law of attraction. etc.

What we are going to explore today is "how to" have karma work for you, rather than against you. As we've discovered, there are various laws of the universe that are in play whether we like it or not. They were in play before we got here, they will be in play after we're gone. Karma is one of them. "Like attracts like."

Let's look at "Like attracts like" for further clarification. Basically what that says is what you put out you get back. If you put out positive energy, taking positive actions, you will get back positive results. Conversely, if you put out negative energy taking negative or no actions, you will attract negative results. Make sense?

Where is energy created? It's created in your observations, thoughts and conversations. Energy can be observed as positive or it can be observed as negative. Just as your observations, thoughts and conversations can be observed as positive or negative.

Imagining for a moment that you want to attract positive results in your life, you need to start the process of positive observations toward your thoughts and positive conversations in order to have the positive results occur. If you have negative observations toward your thoughts and negative conversations, even if you're taking positive actions you won't manifest positive results. "Like attracts like." Your observations, thoughts and conversations (energy) are a lot more powerful than your actions.

It's time to get very conscious to what we are putting out in the universe as far as energy (observations, thoughts and conversations). We need to monitor our thinking and speaking so that it is always in alignment with what we want, and when it's not we need to change it. We need to have our energy on what we can have, and not on what we do not have. We need to be about what we deserve and not what we don't deserve. We need to find the good in our lives and not the bad. "What you look for you will find."

This process is not something that will just happen. In fact it occurs to me that our "thrown to" is to have more negative observations, thoughts and conversations than positive observations, thoughts and conversations. So therefore left to it's own, the mind will almost automatically create negative observations, thoughts, meanings, and conversations. If that's so, and I want you to presume it is, we need to counteract the "thrown to" negative, to a positive and we must do that on a continuous basis.

How do we do that? By positive affirmations. Affirming that something is as you want it in the future, yet you're affirming "as if" it's already occurred. "Calling those things that are not as if they were." By seeing the beauty and greatness of your life and concentrating on that. By raising your mood level to upbeat, joyful, highly optimistic at all times. By taking massive action steps toward what you want in life. By taking those action steps even when you don't want to, especially when you don't want to. By visualizing having what you want even before you have it. By surrounding yourself with upbeat positive people. By putting into your mind empowering motivational information and training, on a continuous basis. etc.

Karma happens whether you like it or not. The good news is, you are in charge of your karma. You can alter the way it's been if you see it's not how you want it to be. Change the inner energy (observations, thoughts and conversations) and the outer energy (results) will be in direct alignment with the inner energy. Use your gift of "Like attracting like" to have all that you want in life. You deserve it!

Monthly Process

1. Make a list of thoughts and conversations that do not serve you.

2. Make a list of the thoughts and conversations you will put in their place to serve positive alignment with your desires.

3. Monitor yourself for 30 days. Write down your daily wins.

Continue Monitoring Daily Wins

Prayer: In affirmative prayer I ask and give thanks to the blessings that surround me, knowing that all energy is divine energy of karmic love and forgiveness, and I am at one with Spirit mind. Amen.

Affirmation: I believe in divine oneness and universal love for nature and all humanity to live in perfect harmony with Spirit.

Spiritual Meditation

Bring to mind a situation within you that you are working through. (Pause) Once you have it in your mind get in a comfortable position and close your eyes, cleansing your mind of all thoughts and allowing a space for lightness and peace….. As you relax into this state you can feel a warm energy that relaxes you even more, dissolving away tension from your head…… down to your toes feeling deeply and deeply relaxed. Head relaxed, shoulders relaxed, chest more relaxed, abdomen very relaxed.   Breathe in from the belly out through the belly,….. your hips are relaxed and legs deeply relaxed. You now feel a greater relaxation as your toes are relaxed….. You are now in a trance-state of deep deep relaxation. As you continue to breathe in through the belly out through the belly, you allow your mind to focus on a thought that you would like to heal within you while you are in this state of deep relaxation….. You are at peace and safe to be receptive now to go into even deeper meditation and visualization.

Take a deep breath through your nose in from your belly up to the top of your head. Hold to the count of 5 … Release it filling your belly back up with air and up to your head again, doing this 3 times, feeling a deeper sense of relaxation… Continue breathing in and out, in from the belly out through the belly… Now slowly count down from 7 to 1 each time going deeper, deeper and deeper, feeling very relaxed…

Now imagine yourself walking through a beautiful garden path, with lush flowers and greenery. You look up at the clouds above and see a beautiful blue sky as the backdrop. You begin to feel a sense of peace and knowingness. As you sense this knowingness you ask the Holy Spirit within you the answer to the situation. Now quiet your mind to allow the answer to come to the surface. Do not judge or analyze the answer, just allow the Energy flow of Spirit to take hold of the question. As you receive the answer, repeat it out loud, stay relaxed and peaceful until you feel it is complete. Take your time and open your eyes when ready, then write down the message you have received.

Insights from Meditation

#11 Monthly Practice

Thoughts Turning Into Feelings

This month let's explore the concept of feelings. How many of you have ever felt happy, sad, lazy, embarrassed, rejected, loved, or not loved? I'd say at one time or another we've all experienced these feelings and many more. In fact, if you think about it we experience numerous feelings throughout every day of our lives. You're probably feeling a certain way as you're reading this.

Where do you think feelings come from? Are they just manifested magically within us? Do they come from our outside occurrences? Are we just at the mercy of our feelings? Not so. Feelings originate from our observations and thoughts. In order to have a feeling we first have to have an observation, thought or conversation. That observation, thought or conversation creates the feeling. If you have a thought of why you should feel rejected you then feel rejected. If you have a thought of why you should feel down you will feel down. If you have a thought of why you should feel happy you will feel happy. Make sense?

If that's so and I want you to hold that it is so, we now have access over our feelings. If we can change our observations, thoughts or conversations we can change our feelings.

How can we change our observations, thoughts and conversations when something we don't like occurs in our life? Very simply by attaching an empowering positive meaning to it. When an occurrence happens it has no meaning. It just is. You then attach your meaning to it, which you observe. You have a choice of whether to observe your meaning as positive and empowering or negative and disempowering. When you create the thought or conversation regarding the meaning, the feeling will follow; positive empowering meaning, positive empowering feeling; negative disempowering meaning, negative disempowering feeling.

This process starts first thing in the morning when you wake up. Waking up has no meaning, it just is. You put the meaning to it. You can either wake up with a conversation of "Good morning God" or a conversation of "Good God it's morning."   Which one do you think will give you the most Power to get up and start your day empowered?

Feelings can be categorized into two sections. The ones that bring you up (empowered) and the ones that bring you down (disempowered). You are going to be much more effective in your life when you are consistently up (empowered). Therefore your observations, thoughts and conversations need to be empowering (positive) rather than disempowering (negative). Because we "make up" all our thoughts and conversations to every event and occurrence in our lives, we get to make the meanings positive and empowering. Then as we keep our power level high we will attract high results in our lives. If we keep our power level low we will attract low results in our lives. Make sense?

If life hasn't already, it will, throw a lot of different situations and occurrences at you. Some of which you weren't intending and certainly didn't want. The things that occur are sometimes inevitable, what you make them mean is your choice. So therefore your feelings become your choice.

When you take on this way of being you will no longer be at the mercy of your feelings. You will be in control of whether you are empowered (up feeling) or disempowered (down feeling). Keep yourself empowered by practicing having empowering observations, thoughts and conversations. Take the actions you need to take to manifest your goals and you will attract to you greater results, and how you feel will be fulfilled through the old saying: "As a man (or woman) thinketh in their heart, so they are." Make your observations and your thoughts manifest great feelings, take the actions consistent with what you want, and you will manifest great results.

Monthly Process

Write 5 or more positive thoughts about your day each evening.

Continued Monthly Process

Prayer: I give thanks and gratitude for my choice of thoughts throughout my day, and pray for universal support to help me observe and perceive a loving universe in which I am part of. Thank you, God. Amen.

Affirmation: I am as God made me, a powerful thought from the Mind of God into manifestation.

Spiritual Meditation

Bring to mind a situation within you that you are working through. (Pause) Once you have it in your mind get in a comfortable position and close your eyes, cleansing your mind of all thoughts and allowing a space for lightness and peace….. As you relax into this state you can feel a warm energy that relaxes you even more, dissolving away tension from your head…… down to your toes feeling deeply and deeply relaxed. Head relaxed, shoulders relaxed, chest more relaxed, abdomen very relaxed.   Breathe in from the belly out through the belly,….. your hips are relaxed and legs deeply relaxed. You now feel a greater relaxation as your toes are relaxed….. You are now in a trance-state of deep deep relaxation. As you continue to breathe in through the belly out through the belly, you allow your mind to focus on a thought that you would like to heal within you while you are in this state of deep relaxation….. You are at peace and safe to be receptive now to go into even deeper meditation and visualization.

Take a deep breath through your nose in from your belly up to the top of your head. Hold to the count of 5 … Release it filling your belly back up with air and up to your head again, doing this 3 times, feeling a deeper sense of relaxation… Continue breathing in and out, in from the belly out through the belly… Now slowly count down from 7 to 1 each time going deeper, deeper and deeper, feeling very relaxed…

Imagine lying on a blanket on a beautiful warm summer night. You hear the sound of crickets and see fire flies in the air. As you look up to the sky you see what looks like a billion stars. You also see the Milky Way and the Big Dipper. The sweet aroma of gardenias fills the air, as you lie there. You are very, very deeply relaxed. You begin to count down from 7 to 1,feeling very relaxed … Have your mind start to play back the moments of your life, from present day to childhood. As you do this take your time exploring your thoughts at each stage of your life. No need to analyze it, just allow it to flow to the surface and out to the sky above, allowing those thoughts to unite with the stars. As you empty out those thoughts you remain very deeply, deeply relaxed. Count down from 7 to 1, then begin again thinking of your life from present day to childhood. This time think the thoughts and feelings of the Spiritual You that you know yourself to be. Take time as you create your thoughts and feelings about your life, staying very relaxed... you slowly bring yourself back to the present with a smile. When you feel you are complete, open your eyes and record what positive thoughts and feelings you have created in each phase of your life.

Insights from Meditation

#12 Monthly Practice

Observation Equals Manifestation

We are going to explore the process of "observing." What I mean by that is; How we perceive things, are how things are for us. For example: If you observe your job as difficult, hard, unchallenging, or boring, that is how your job will show up for you. If you observe your relationship as combative, chaotic, unfulfilling, unloving, that is how your relationship will show up for you. If you observe change as fearful, unsettling, uncomfortable, scary, challenging, that is how change will show up for you and you'll stay stuck somewhere you don't want to be.

How we observe things or say that they are has us "act as if" it's true, and as we "act as if" they're true, we will generate the "evidence" to support that truth, that we in fact had "made up" in the first place. Every part of our mental observation is made up. It may not seem to you that it's made up, yet it is. Think about it for a moment. If you're observing a thought about something that may happen in the future, doesn't it have to be made up. The only thing that is real is what is actually happening at the present moment. Everything else is "made up." Even the things that may happen to us, we make up our meanings to what happens. Not that we make up what happens, we make up what we make what happens mean. For example: Let's say you're stuck in traffic. That has "no meaning," "it just is." Not that you're not stuck in traffic, because you are, but everything after that is "made up" by your observation of traffic.

We have two choices as to what we make things mean. We can make them mean something negative or we can make them mean something positive. How do we determine what is negative and what is positive? Negative moves us away from what we want. Positive moves us toward what we want. If we are making something mean negative, we then start acting "as if" it's true and we create more of the negatives in our lives. If we make something mean positive we start acting "as if" positive is true and we will create more positives in our lives. For

242

example: If you are in sales and you have prospecting calls to make and you make them "mean" negative (hard, I may get rejected, they're not interested, I may be bothering them, they don't want to talk to a salesperson, etc.), you will start "acting as if" it's true and you will create the evidence (not a successful call) to be right about what you "made up" about the prospecting call in the first place. By the same token, if you observe prospecting calls mean something positive (I am going to assist someone in meeting their needs, I have a valuable service or product for them, my product or service will make their lives better, I owe it to them to call them to make them aware of what I am offering, I'm helping them fulfill a need, etc.), you will then be observing the positive as the truth, thereby having a more positive experience on the call, making an appointment or making happen whatever you were calling for.

The way to use observation to your advantage is for you to determine what you want the outcome of your observation to be manifested before you start to take the action and to continuously tell yourself (positively affirming) that which you want to manifest "as if" it's already happened. Such as: "I am abundant financially. I am healthy and fit. I have a great marriage, or relationship. I have the sale I am calling on. My life is easy and effortless. I am at peace within. I am enjoying this present experience." etc. Whatever it is you want to create, observe it "as if" it's already created. Then take the actions it will take to manifest that which you want to create, and you will achieve many more of your goals, dreams, and aspirations, with more fun and ease.

Monthly Process

Write 5 observations per day where you observed an area before you went into automatic reaction and generated a positive manifestation.

Continued Monthly Process

Prayer: I give thanks and gratitude for the ability to observe my world into creation, that through my thoughts I can manifest peace, harmony and love for myself and all Spiritual beings.   That as a positive observer I become a positive participator. Thank you God. Amen

Affirmation: I am the Co-Creator of the world I observe and choose to Create Peace, Harmony and Love.

Spiritual Meditation

Bring to mind a situation within you that you are working through. (Pause) Once you have it in your mind get in a comfortable position and close your eyes, cleansing your mind of all thoughts and allowing a space for lightness and peace….. As you relax into this state you can feel a warm energy that relaxes you even more, dissolving away tension from your head…… down to your toes feeling deeply and deeply relaxed. Head relaxed, shoulders relaxed, chest more relaxed, abdomen very relaxed.   Breathe in from the belly out through the belly,….. your hips are relaxed and legs deeply relaxed. You now feel a greater relaxation as your toes are relaxed….. You are now in a trance-state of deep deep relaxation. As you continue to breathe in through the belly out through the belly, you allow your mind to focus on a thought that you would like to heal within you while you are in this state of deep relaxation….. You are at peace and safe to be receptive now to go into even deeper meditation and visualization.
Take a deep breath through your nose in from your belly up to the top of your head. Hold to the count of 5 … Release it filling your belly back up with air and up to your head again, doing this 3 times, feeling a deeper sense of relaxation… Continue breathing in and out, in from the belly out through the belly… Now slowly count down from 7 to 1 each time going deeper, deeper and deeper, feeling very relaxed….

Now imagine yourself at an ancient coliseum made of stone. It is empty and you are the only one there. The sky is grey and you hear a loud sound of thunder and see lightning as it begins to rain, but you are not afraid for you are well tucked away in a cove of the coliseum. As you look around you decide to create a different view of this coliseum. You first start by observing the sky and think it to be clear. As you do this the clouds start to part, the lightning stops and the rain is no longer falling from the sky. What you observe is a beautiful bright blue sky with a bright rainbow going across the coliseum. It is such a breath taking sight that you want to share it with others. As you keep your observation on the beauty of the moment you observe people coming into the coliseum with bright smiles on their faces and amazement at the beauty surrounding them. You then observe the entire coliseum filled with people of different cultures and skin color, speaking in different languages but understanding each other through a smile, laugh or gesture. You observe that these people appear different, yet they are very much the same Spiritual beings as yourself. Once they are all seated you observe that from the middle of the coliseum toward the back of it, a gate opens and you observe a feeling of positive loving energy illuminating from the gate outward toward the coliseum. You know at that moment, who is descending from the gate. Take your time to observe your thoughts on who is appearing and what Spiritual message they have to give. When you are ready open your eyes and record what you saw and what was said.

Insights from Meditation

Closing

Here it is; a road map toward your destination to Rome (meaning Home), back to the center of where you came from. No matter what modality you choose, it will always be up to the you that you are from within, which is the Center of God. That is where we will find our answers to who we are and what is the purpose of our life. It is to find our center and assist humanity along the way to find their center. We can't do it for them; we can only assist them through first assisting ourselves. As one mind is healed from *split mind* thinking another will be healed from *split mind* thinking, and on and on it will be paid forward until the awakening of Christ Consciousness has found its Center as a whole Universal oneness, and doubts of dualities will be set aside because of the knowledge of knowing what we know, that duality lives in an illusionary world and that truth lives in the world of Oneness. Through the correction of the *split mind*, choosing Spirit over ego will catapult our journey back to our true identity and Christ consciousness, the highest level of super-consciousness where all exists as one non-dualistic concept; wholeness.

Start and stay on the journey through daily practice of the present, which is the gift of life. Continue to monitor where you put your thoughts, ego side or Spirit side, using your inner gauge and how you feel when you select where you place your inner thought that then becomes an idea, then an emotion, to manifestation.   You can manifest your heart's desire through this method of right mind thinking, as God intended for us before we bought into the world of illusion. Now is the time to take charge of your observations of your thoughts that are perceived through the past and brought to the present, in order to extend to the future. So ask yourself what future you would desire to have and what thoughts support it toward the action required to manifestation.

The more you realize Spirit mind thinking is required the easier it will get. Before we try to manage the world's false illusion of consciousness we must first learn to manage our own false illusionary consciousness of who we think ourselves to be through ego and realize and accept ourselves as pure Spirit with full consciousness, love, forgiveness and universal oneness.

Through partnership we can heal one another from the world of illusion. When we become conscious of another, we become conscious of ourselves by looking at the mirror they are reflecting within us. You can't see it unless you know it. So, we can see and perceive ego thoughts and look to see where it lives within us. Or, we can perceive love and forgiveness and look to see where that lives within us, and operate from that space to help heal our thoughts and the thoughts of humanity.

The illusionary world is made up by thoughts and images that have been given meaning. If you are not content with the image then change the thought about it. If our imaging is created with Spirit thoughts rather than ego thoughts we would have a universe in which Utopia could be reached from within. By discovering and healing our subconscious thoughts we become a continuation of Christ consciousness all around us.

Blessings,
See you in Rome (Home)
Reverend Mercedes Pepe, O. M. C.

This is not the end of the road, it is the beginning!
Mercedes Pepe, O.M.C.

Mercedes Pepe, O.M.C.

About the Author

Reverend Mercedes Pepe, O.M.C. is an Ordained Ministerial Counselor, member of Coachville University and is certified at level III in working with the clarity meter. She offers the opportunity of awaking Spiritually, through Pathways of Light Courses, both in groups and through correspondence by phone. She is also available to help people access their inner guidance to heal their mind through one on one Spiritual Counseling. Mercedes is certified and authorized to assist in couples relationships. She is a Master Reiki Healer and a certified Hypnotherapist. Mercedes is available to work one on one utilizing this workbook, via the telephone utilizing her Spiritual Counseling and trained Processing skills.

She can be contacted through her website: www.powertechnology.org
Power Technology is a Success/Life Coaching company est. 1992.

251